lonely planet

POCKET BARCELONA

TOP SIGHTS • LOCAL EXPERIENCES

SALLY DAVIES, CATHERINE LE NEVEZ

Contents

Plan Your Trip

The roof of Casa Batlló (p114)
KRISKELLY49/BUDGET TRAVEL ©

Explore Barcelona 37

Survival Guide 174

Special Features

Welcome to Barcelona

A thoroughly captivating city, Barcelona is a whirlwind of madcap Modernista architecture, sun-kissed beaches and lamplit medieval streets hiding brilliantly creative dining and drinking dens. The storied Catalan capital holds ancient Roman ruins and artistic masterpieces of the modern era, Gothic palaces and retro cocktail bars – and one of the world's most venerated football stadiums.

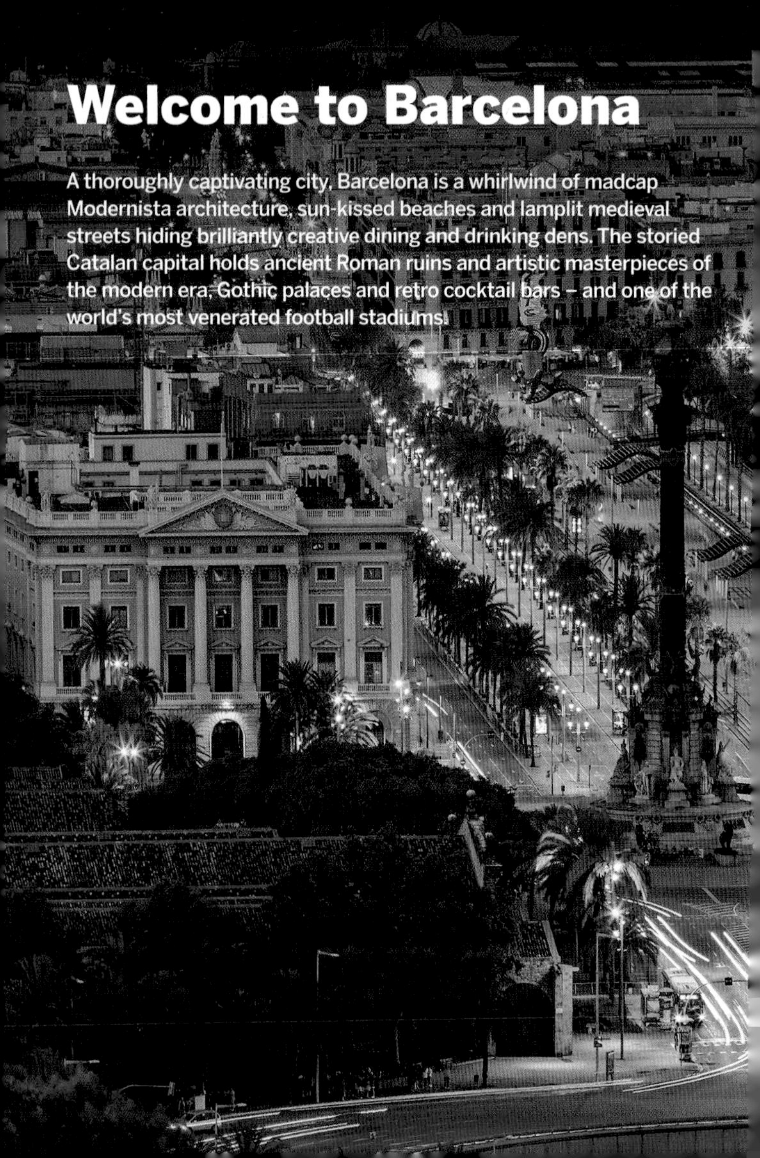

Aerial view over Barceloneta (p93)
KAVALENKAVA/SHUTTERSTOCK ©

Top Sights

ALESSANDRO COLLE/SHUTTERSTOCK ©

La Sagrada Família

Spain's most visited monument. **p124**

MARC SOLER/ALAMY STOCK PHOTO ©

Museu Picasso

Showcase for Picasso's early work. **p74**

Camp Nou

Barcelona's hallowed football ground. **p146**

NATURSPORTS/SHUTTERSTOCK ©

La Rambla

Legendary mile-long boulevard. **p40**

MIHAI-BOGDAN LAZAR/SHUTTERSTOCK ©

Park Güell

Gaudí's fantastically landscaped hilltop park. **p130**

LUCIANO MORTULA/SHUTTERSTOCK ©

ALLIK/SHUTTERSTOCK ©

Mercat de la Boqueria

Europe's greatest food market. **p60**

NEIL SETCHFIELD/LONELY PLANET ©

Fundació Joan Miró

Showcases Joan Miró's seminal works. **p160**

Museu Nacional d'Art de Catalunya

Art in palatial surroundings. **p156**

ANDY CALEY/SHUTTERSTOCK ©

Basílica de Santa Maria del Mar

Fine Catalan Gothic church. **p78**

FARAZ BUTTE/500PX ©

FRANKI1/SHUTTERSTOCK ©

La Catedral

Soaring, Disney-like cathedral. **p44**

IMAGE COURTESY OF CATALUNYA LA PEDRERA FOUNDATION

La Pedrera

A madcap Gaudí masterpiece. **p108**

Eating

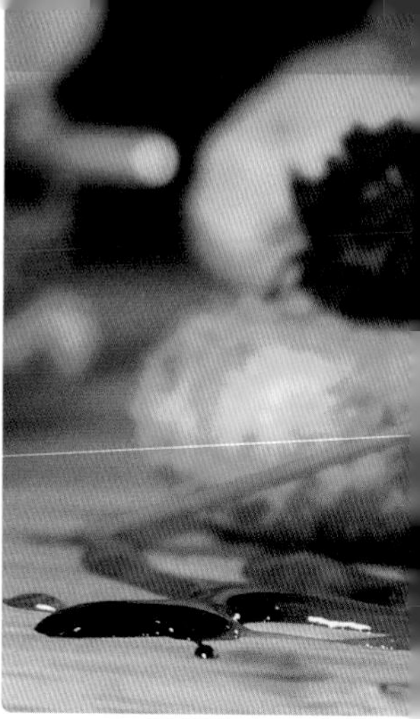

Barcelona has a celebrated food scene fuelled by a combination of world-class chefs, imaginative recipes and magnificent ingredients fresh from farms and the sea. Catalan culinary masterminds like Ferran Adrià have become international icons, reinventing the world of haute cuisine, while classic old-world Catalan recipes continue to shine in dining rooms across the city.

New Catalan Cuisine

Avant-garde chefs have made Catalonia famous throughout the world for their food laboratories and commitment to food as art. Here the notion of gourmet cuisine is deconstructed as chefs transform liquids and solid foods into foams, create 'ice cream' of classic ingredients by means of liquid nitrogen, freeze-dry foods to make concentrated powders and employ spherification to create unusual and artful morsels. Invention is the keystone of this technique.

Classic Catalan Cuisine

Traditional Catalan recipes showcase the great produce of the Mediterranean: fish, prawns, cuttlefish, clams, pork, rabbit, game, first-rate olive oil, peppers and loads of garlic. Classic dishes also feature unusual pairings (seafood with meat, fruit with fowl) such as cuttlefish with chickpeas, cured ham with caviar, rabbit with prawns, or goose with pears.

Tapas

Tapas, those bite-sized morsels of joy, are not a typical Catalan concept, but tapas bars are nonetheless found all across the city. Most open earlier than restaurants – typically around 7pm – making them a good pre-dinner (or instead-of-dinner) option. Some open from lunch and stay open without a break until late evening.

JUANSALVADOR/SHUTTERSTOCK ©

Best Catalan

Vivanda Magnificent Catalan cooking with year-round garden dining. (p151)

La Panxa del Bisbe Creative sharing plates on a quiet Gràcia street. (p131)

Cafè de l'Acadèmia High-quality dishes that never disappoint. (p53)

Can Culleretes The city's oldest restaurant, with great-value traditional dishes. (p54)

Can Lluís Loved by Catalans for its great-value daily *menú*. (p68)

Best Cafes

Bar del Convent Great terrace in a former cloister. (p89)

Café Godot Friendly and easy-going, with tasty snacks and mains. (p137)

La Granja Best place in town for a hot chocolate. (p55)

La Nena Kid-friendly cafe in Gràcia. (p137)

Cafè de l'Òpera Stop in for late-night snacks on La Rambla. (p41)

Best Tapas

El 58 French-owned space on the newly hip Rambla del Poblenou. (p101)

Quimet i Quimet Mouth-watering morsels served to a standing crowd. (p171)

Palo Cortao A new star in Poble Sec with outstanding sharing plates. (p172)

Tapas 24 Everyone's favourite gourmet tapas bar. (p118)

Top Tip

The *menú del día*, a full set meal with water or wine, is a great way to cap prices at lunchtime. They start from around €11 and can go as high as €25 for more elaborate offerings.

Barcelona on a Plate

Salsa Romesco

Typical accompaniment to *mar i muntanya* (meat and seafood combination) dishes.
The nuts can be almonds, hazel-nuts, pine nuts or a combination.
Bread or toast is used as a thickener.
Tastes great over grilled fish.
Traditionally made with dried *cuerno de cabra* ('goat horn') peppers.

★ Top Five for Romesco Dishes

El 58 (p101) This French-Catalan place serves imaginative, beautifully prepared tapas dishes.

Vivanda (p151) Magnificent Catalan cooking with dishes showcasing seasonal fare.

Belmonte (p54) This tiny tapas joint in the southern reaches of Barri Gòtic whips up beautifully prepared small plates.

Casa Delfín (p87) A culinary delight, this place is everything you dream of when you think of Catalan (and Mediterranean) cooking.

El Glop (p138) The secret to this raucous restaurant is no-nonsense, slap-up meals.

A Catalan Classic

This classic Catalan sauce pervades the region's cuisine, popping up in numerous dishes as an accompaniment to roasted vegetables, grilled meats and fish. It's a rich, garlicky, nutty combination based on peppers and tomatoes. A thickened version, *salvitxada*, is the de rigueur dipping accompaniment for the late winter barbecues of *calçots*, the delicious leek-like onions beloved of Catalans.

Calçots with romesco sauce

Drinking & Nightlife

Barcelona is a nightlife-lovers' town, with an enticing spread of candlelit wine bars, old-school taverns, stylish lounges and kaleidoscopic nightclubs where the party continues until daybreak. For something a little more sedate, the city's atmospheric cafes and teahouses make a fine retreat when the skies turn grey.

Bars & Lounges

Barcelona has a dizzying assortment of bars – candlelit, mural-covered chambers in the medieval quarter, antique-filled converted shops and buzzing Modernista spaces are all part of the scene. Whether you're in the mood to drink with hipsters (try Sant Antoni), the bohemian crowd (El Raval) or young expats (Gràcia), you'll find a scene that suits in Barcelona.

Wine & Cava Bars

A growing number of wine bars scattered around the city showcase the great produce from Spain and beyond. Vine-minded spots serve a huge selection of wines by the glass, and a big part of the experience is having a few bites while you drink.

Cava bars tend to be more about the festive ambience than the actual drinking of *cava*, most of which is produced in Catalonia's Penedès region. At the more famous *cava* bars you'll have to nudge your way through the garrulous crowds and enjoy your bubbly standing up.

Clubs

Barcelona's *discotecas* (clubs) are at their best from Thursday to Saturday. Indeed, many open only on these nights. A surprising variety of spots lurk in the old-town labyrinth, ranging from plush former dance halls to grungy subterranean venues that fill to capacity.

Along the waterfront it's another story. At Port Olímpic, sun-scorched crowds of visiting yachties mix it up with tourists and a few locals at noisy, back-to-back dance bars right on the waterfront.

TRAVEL PICTURES/ALAMY STOCK PHOTO ©

Best Cocktails

Paradiso Walk through a fridge to this glam speakeasy. (p86)

Balius Beautifully mixed elixirs in Poblenou. (p104)

Elephanta The place to linger over a creative concoction. (p140)

Dry Martini Expertly made cocktails in a classy setting. (p121)

Boadas An iconic drinking den that's been going strong since the 1930s. (p55)

Best Wine Bars

Viblioteca A small modern space famed for its wine (and cheese) selections. (p139)

Perikete A large and lively new wine bar in Barceloneta. (p102)

Monvínic With a staggering 3000 varieties of wines, you won't lack for options. (p120)

La Vinya del Senyor Long wine list and tables in the shadow of Basílica de Santa Maria del Mar. (p79)

Best Dancing

Marula Cafè Barri Gòtic favourite for its lively dance floor. (p55)

Sala Apolo Gorgeous dance-hall with varied programme of electro, funk and more. (p165)

Moog A small Raval club that draws a fun, dance-loving crowd. (p70)

Antilla BCN The top name in town for salsa lovers. (p122)

City Hall A legendary Eixample dance club. (p122)

Top Tip

Look out for club flyers in shops and bars, which often provide discounted entry. If you arrive at a club before 1am, you're likely to get free admission – although it may be a little lonely in there.

Barcelona in a Glass

Cava

Cava consumption rockets up at Christmas time

Brut Nature, Extra Brut and Brut are the driest styles

Normally made from Macabeu, Parellada and Xarel·lo grapes

Reserva and Gran Reserva wines have extra bottle age

Dulce and Semi Seco are the sweet styles

Cava also comes in rosé

★ Best Places to Drink *Cava*

El Xampanyet (p89) Nothing has changed for decades in this, one of the city's best-known cava bars.

Can Paixano (p103) This lofty cava bar has long been run on a winning formula: the standard tipple is bubbly rosé in elegant little glasses.

Perikete (p102) Since opening in 2017, this fabulous wine bar has been jam-packed with locals.

Viblioteca (p139) The real speciality here is wine, and you can choose from 150 mostly local labels, many of them available by the glass.

¡Salud!

Produced in the vineyards of the Penedès region, *cava* is Spain's most prominent sparkling wine. It undergoes a creation process similar to that of champagne and comes in varying grades of dryness or sweetness.

Sangria, the refreshing summery blend of wine, fruit, sugar and a dash of something harder, is given a twist in Catalonia by using *cava* instead of cheap red.

White sangria ready to drink

Shopping

Across Ciutat Vella (Barri Gòtic, El Raval and La Ribera), L'Eixample and Gràcia is spread a thick mantle of boutiques, historic shops, original one-off stores, gourmet corners, wine dens and designer labels. You name it, you'll find it here.

Boutique Barcelona

The heart of the Barri Gòtic has always been busy with small-scale merchants, but the area has come crackling to life since the mid-1990s. Some of the most curious old shops, such as purveyors of hats and candles, lurk in the narrow streets around Plaça de Sant Jaume. Carrer d'Avinyó has become a minor young-fashion boulevard, and antique shops line Carrer de la Palla and Carrer dels Banys Nous.

La Ribera is a gourmet's delight. Great old shops deal in speciality foodstuffs, from coffee and chocolate to roasted nuts. Amid such wonderful aromas, fashion and design stores cater to the multitude of fashionistas in the *barrio*.

Markets

Barcelona's food markets are some of the best in Europe – just think of the inviting, glistening, aromatic and voluptuous offerings to be savoured in Mercat de la Boqueria (p60) or Mercat de Santa Caterina (p84). Every neighbourhood has its own central market, full of seasonal offers.

Several flea markets, like Els Encants Vells (p105), offer the opportunity to browse and enjoy the local buzz, and perhaps even find a good bargain.

Vintage Fashion

El Raval is best for vintage fashion. You'll discover old-time stores that are irresistible to browsers, and a colourful array of affordable, mostly secondhand clothes boutiques, especially along Carrer de la Riera Baixa, which plays host to '70s threads and military cast-offs. Carrer dels Tallers attracts a growing number of clothing and shoe shops (although music

NEJRON PHOTO/SHUTTERSTOCK ©

remains its core business). Small galleries, designer shops and arty bookshops huddle together along the streets running east of the MACBA (p65).

Best Fashion

Coquette Offbeat women's clothes that share an ethereal elegance. (p91)

Holala! Plaza Today vintage is the new designer, and nowhere has a better selection than Holala! (p71)

Bagués-Masriera Exquisite jewellery from a company with a long tradition. (p123)

Custo Barcelona Quirky, colourful clothes that are not for the shy. (p91)

Loisaida Cute, smart and somewhat retro clothing for men and women. (p91)

Best Markets

Mercat de la Boqueria The quintessential Barcelona food market. (p60)

Mercat de Santa Caterina A colourful alternative to La Boqueria, with fewer crowds and lower prices. (p84)

Els Encants Vells A sprawling flea market in a spanking new building. (p105)

El Bulevard dels Antiquaris A labyrinth of tiny antique shops that merits a morning's browsing. (p123)

Best Souvenirs & Gifts

Born Centre de Cultura i Memòria The gift shop at this exhibition space stocks tasteful, well-made souvenirs, and books about the city. (p180)

Les Topettes Creams, oils, perfumes and soaps that look every bit as tantalising as they smell. (p70)

Sabater Hermanos Divinely fragranced shop selling handmade soaps in pretty gift boxes. (p56)

Top Tip

Spain's only surviving department store is **El Corte Inglés** (p122). An enormous main branch towers over Plaça de Catalunya and covers all manner of things – books, music, food, fashion, jewellery, toys, technology and homeware. There are branches across town.

Top Barcelona Souvenirs

TIM E WHITE/ALAMY STOCK PHOTO ©

Build a Gaudí

We might not have the maestro's imagination, but by damn we can reconstruct his buildings in miniature. Available in most Gaudí buildings and museum shops.

Fashion

Quality threads can be had all over town, but best seek out a small local design boutique to ensure you head back wearing something unique.

CATWALKER/SHUTTERSTOCK ©

NITO/SHUTTERSTOCK ©

Cured Meats

Instead of *jamón*, go for local sausage such as *fuet* or *botifarra*. It's best bought in one of the market halls. They'll vacuum-pack it for you.

CHARNSITR/SHUTTERSTOCK ©

FC Barcelona Gear

Sure, you can buy a rip-off Messi shirt in any market in the world, but the real deal plus harder-to-come-by Barça mementoes are in their official shops.

CARLOSANDRESANTOS/GETTY IMAGES ©

Wine

Look for something you can't get back home – some small-producer Catalan red, or a hard-to-get *cava* (sparkling wine). Shops in La Ribera have ample supplies.

Architecture

EQROY/SHUTTERSTOCK ©

Famed for its architectural treasures, Barcelona has striking Gothic cathedrals, fantastical Modernista creations and avant-garde works from more recent days. The city's great building boom first began in the late Middle Ages, when Barcelona was seat of the Catalan empire. The late 19th century was another time of great ferment, when the city began expanding beyond its medieval confines.

Best Gothic Giants

La Catedral The old city's Gothic centrepiece, at once extravagant and sombre. (p44)

Basílica de Santa Maria del Mar Arguably the high point of Catalan Gothic. (p78)

Basílica de Santa Maria del Pi A 14th-century jewel with a dazzling rose window. (p86)

Museu Marítim In the former Gothic shipyards just off the seaward end of La Rambla. (p98)

Museu-Monestir de Pedralbes A 14th century monastery with a superb three-level cloister. (p149)

Museu Picasso Rare surviving examples of Gothic mansions, now converted artfully into exhibition space. (p179)

Best of Gaudí

La Sagrada Família Gaudí's unfinished symphony. (p124)

La Pedrera Showpiece Gaudí apartment building with an otherworldly roof. (p108)

Casa Batlló An eye-catching facade, with an astonishing interior to match. (p114)

Palau Güell Gaudí's only building in the old part of town. (p65)

Park Güell Gaudí's playfulness in full swing. (p130)

Best of the Modernista Rest

Palau de la Música Catalana Breathtaking concert hall by Lluís Domènech i Montaner. (p84)

Casa Amatller Josep Puig i Cadafalch's neighbour to Casa Batlló with gabled roof. (p114)

Casa Lleó Morera Ornate facade of dancing nymphs, rooftop cupolas and interior stained glass. (p115)

Fundació Antoni Tàpies A brick and iron-framed masterpiece designed by Domènech i Montaner (p179)

Recinte Modernista de Sant Pau Gilded pavilions north of La Sagrada Família by Domènech i Montaner. (p114)

Palau del Baró Quadras Stained-glass and neo-Gothic flourishes by Puig i Cadalfalch. (p117)

Art & Design

BLACK CLOUD BY CARLOS AMORALES, AT CENTRE DE CULTURA CONTEMPORÀNIA DE BARCELONA (CCCB)
HEMIS/ALAMY STOCK PHOTO ©

Barcelona has for centuries been a canvas for great artists – its streets, parks and galleries are littered with the signatures of artists past and present. From Modernista sculptors, such as Josep Llimona, to international and home-grown stars such as Roy Lichtenstein and Joan Miró, they've all left their mark.

Best 20th-Century Art & Design

Museu Picasso A journey through Picasso's work before cubism took over his life. (p179)

Fundació Joan Miró Joan Miró's portfolio, from his formative years to later works. (p179)

Fundació Antoni Tàpies A selection of Tàpies' works and contemporary art exhibitions. (p179)

Museu Nacional d'Art de Catalunya Modern Catalan art on the upstairs floor of Barcelona's premier art museum. (p179)

MACBA Fabulous rotating collection of local and international contemporary art. (p179)

Fundació Suñol Rich private collection of photography, sculpture and paintings (some by Picasso). (p117)

Centre de Cultura Contemporània de Barcelona High-class rotating exhibitions, often focusing on photography. (p179)

CaixaForum Dynamic artistic space in a beautifully converted Modernista building. (p168)

Museu del Modernisme Barcelona Modernistas (including Gaudí) turn their attention to home furnishings. (p117)

Best Street Art

Homenatge a la Barceloneta Rebecca Horn's tribute to Barceloneta's pre-Olympics waterfront culture. (p102)

Mosaïc de Miró The work of Barcelona's artistic icon adorns the footpath of La Rambla. (p43)

Gaudí's Lamp Posts One of Gaudí's earliest commissions in the Barri Gòtic's Plaça Reial.

Parks & Beaches

IAKOV FILIMONOV/SHUTTERSTOCK ©

The tight tangle of streets that constitutes Barcelona's old town can feel claustrophobic at times. But once you move beyond, Barcelona opens up as a city of light and space – its parks, gardens and long stretches of sand bequeath the city an unmistakably Mediterranean air.

Best Parks & Gardens

Park Güell Everybody's favourite public park, where zany Gaudí flourishes meet landscape gardening. (p130)

Parc de la Ciutadella Home to parliament, a zoo, public art and abundant shade. (p86)

Jardins de Mossèn Cinto de Verdaguer Gentle, sloping Montjuïc gardens devoted to bulbs and water lilies. (p163)

Jardí Botànic More than 40,000 plants faithful to a loosely defined Mediterranean theme. (p169)

Jardins de Mossèn Costa i Llobera An exotic stand of tropical and desert flora. (p170)

Jardins del Mirador Good views and a handful of snack bars below the castle. (p163)

Best Beaches

Platja de Nova Icària Perhaps the loveliest of Barcelona's city beaches, located just beyond Port Olímpic.

Platja de Somorrostro Plenty of sand and more of a locals' beach than others.

Platja de la Barceloneta Family-friendly beach where Barceloneta meets the sea. (p104)

Tours

There are many ways to get a more in-depth look at the city, whether on a specialised walking tour through the Ciutat Vella (Old City), on a bicycle excursion around the city centre or on a hop-on, hop-off bus tour all across town.

ANAMARIA MEJIA/SHUTTERSTOCK ©

Best Tours

Barcelona Walking Tours (☎93 285 38 34; www.barcelonaturisme.com; Plaça de Catalunya 17; M Catalunya) The tourist office runs 17 themed walking tours that focus on the Barri Gòtic, Picasso's Barcelona, Modernisme and the city's food culture.

Bike Tours Barcelona (☎93 268 21 05; www.biketoursbarcelona.com; Carrer de l'Esparteria 3; per person €25; ⌚10am-7pm; M Jaume I) One of numerous operators offering three-hour tours of the Barri Gòtic, waterfront, La Sagrada Família and other Gaudí landmarks. Turn up outside the tourist office on Plaça de Sant Jaume; check the website for departure times.

Las Golondrinas (☎93 442 31 06; www.lasgolondrinas.com; Moll de las Drassanes; adult/child port tour €7.50/2.80, catamaran tour €15/5.50; M Drassanes) A seaborne perspective of the city with a jaunt around the harbour in the 'swallow boats'.

My Favourite Things (☎637 265405; www.myft.net; tours from €26) Offers tours for no more than 10 participants based on numerous themes: anything from design to food. Other activities include flamenco and salsa classes, and bicycle rides in and out of Barcelona.

Bus Turístic (☎93 298 70 00; www.barcelonabusturistic.cat; adult/child 1 day €29/16, 2 days €39/16; ⌚9am-8pm) This hop-on, hop-off service covers virtually all of the city's main sights. Audioguides (in 10 languages) provide running commentary on the 44 stops on the three different circuits. Each of the two main circuits takes around two hours.

Ruta del Modernisme For a self-guided tour that leads past 115 Modernista buildings, pick up this book and map (€12) at the main tourist office on Plaça de Catalunya.

For Kids

From street performers who strut their stuff the length of La Rambla to art and architecture that looks like it emerged from a child's imagination, the sheer theatre of Barcelona's streets is a source of endless fascination for kids. Throw in an abundance of child-centric attractions (including beaches, pools and parks) and this is one city that

Child-Friendly Culture

One of the great things about Barcelona is the inclusion of children in many apparently adult activities. Going out to eat or sipping a beer on a late summer evening at a *terraza* needn't mean leaving children with minders. Locals take their kids out all the time and it's not unusual to see all ages, from toddlers to grandparents, enjoying the city until well into the night. A good starting point for what Barcelona has to offer for children can be found at www.kidsinbarcelona.com; its child-friendly listings are updated regularly.

Practical Matters

Most of the mid- and upper-range hotels in Barcelona can organise a babysitting service. Many hotels use **5 Serveis** (☎93 412 56 76; www.5serveis.com; Carrer de Pelai 50; Ⓜ Catalunya), which you can also contact directly. It has multilingual babysitters (*canguros*). Expect to pay at least €10 an hour plus a taxi fare home for the babysitter. If you're willing to let your kid share your bed, you won't incur a supplement in hotels. Extra beds usually (though not always) incur a €20 to €30 charge.

Top Tips

Adjust your children to Barcelona time (ie late nights), otherwise they'll miss half of what's worth seeing. Ask the local tourist office for the nearest children's playgrounds.

CATARINA BELOVA/SHUTTERSTOCK ©

Best Attractions

L'Aquàrium One of Spain's best aquariums, with a shark tunnel and 11,000 fish. (p98)

Beaches Plenty of sand and gentle waters within walking distance.

Poble Espanyol A village in miniature that's guaranteed to capture the kids' attention. (p169)

Teleférico del Puerto Exhilarating cable car that feels like a fairground ride. (p170)

Parc de la Ciutadella Central Barcelona's largest park with ample space to play. (p86)

L'Anella Olímpica & Estadi Olímpic Swim the same pool as Olympic greats. (p170)

Camp Nou The football-mad kid will never forget a visit here. (p25)

Best Museums

Museu de Cera Wax museum, complete with fairy-tale forest and time travel. (p53)

Museu Marítim Model ships, rafts and tall tales of the sea. (p98)

Castell de Montjuïc Patrol the city ramparts. (p170)

Museu Olímpic i de l'Esport Sporty kids will love it. (p170)

Best for Fertile Imaginations

Park Güell Animals in glittering colours and *Hansel and Gretel*–like gatehouses. (p130)

Casa Batlló Architecture made for kids. (p114)

La Sagrada Família Castle-like structure that seems to spring from a medieval legend. (p124)

Fundació Joan Miró Children can relate to the childlike shapes and strong colours. (p179)

Museums

MARTIN HUGHES/LONELY PLANET ©

With such a rich heritage of art and architecture, few cities rival Barcelona's array of world-class museums. As always in Spain, the line between a museum and an art gallery is deliciously blurred; in this section we've concentrated on traditional museums that take you for a ride through the history of Catalonia and beyond, with detours into the world of art.

Best Journeys Through History

Museu d'Història de Barcelona Rich Roman ruins and Gothic architecture. (p180)

Museu d'Història de Catalunya A wonderfully composed ode to Catalan history. (p98)

Museu Marítim Barcelona as Mediterranean port city in the Gothic former shipyards. (p98)

Camp Nou Experience Learn about the history of FC Barcelona, including dark episodes that include assassination and kidnapping. (p25)

Museu Etnològic Discover Catalan traditions and rituals. (p168)

MUHBA Refugi 307 Revisit wartime Barcelona in this evocative network of air-raid shelters. (p168)

Museu-Monestir de Pedralbes A window on monastic life and marvellous Gothic cloister. (p149)

Best Art History Museums

Museu Nacional d'Art de Catalunya Breathtaking Romanesque art and a peerless portfolio of Catalan artists. (p179)

Museu Frederic Marès Outstanding repository of Spanish sculpture, with Romanesque art the star. (p52)

Museu Gaudí Step inside Gaudí's mind and workshop with drawings and scale models. (p124)

Casa-Museu Gaudí Gaudí's one-time home in Park Güell. (p131)

Museu Olímpic i de l'Esport Fascinating survey of Olympian history. (p170)

LGBTIQ+

ALEXANDROS MICHAILIDIS/SHUTTERSTOCK ©

With a busy gay and lesbian scene, this is one of the most gay-friendly cities in southern Europe. The bulk of the action happens in 'Gaixample', the five or six blocks of L'Eixample bounded by Gran Via de les Corts Catalanes, Carrer de Balmes, Carrer del Consell de Cent and Carrer de Casanova.

Best Bars

La Chapelle (☎93 453 30 76; Carrer de Muntaner 67; ⏰4pm-2am Sun-Thu, to 2.30am Fri & Sat; **M** Universitat) Relaxed meeting place with provocative religious decor that welcomes all.

Aire (Sala Diana; ☎93 487 83 42; www.grupoarena.com; Carrer de la Diputació 233; cover Fri/Sat €5/6; ⏰11pm-2.30am Thu-Sat; **M** Passeig de Gràcia) Popular spot for lesbians with a spacious dance floor.

Átame (☎93 421 41 33; Carrer del Consell de Cent 257; ⏰7.30pm-2.30am Tue, 8.30pm-2.30am Wed, Thu & Sun, 8.30pm-3am Fri & Sat; **M** Universitat) Chat over drinks early, stay late as things heat up.

Punto BCN (☎93 451 91 52; www.grupoarena.com; Carrer de Muntaner 65; ⏰6pm-2.30am Sun-Thu, to 3am Fri & Sat; **M** Universitat) A two-level bar with a good mix of ages and creeds.

Bacon Bear (☎93 431 00 00; Carrer de Casanova 64; ⏰6pm-2.30am Mon-Thu, to 3am Fri & Sat, to 2.30am Sun; **M** Urgell) Burly folk and their admirers.

Best Clubs

Arena Madre (☎93 487 83 42; www.grupoarena.com; Carrer de Balmes 32; cover Sun-Fri €6, Sat €12; ⏰12.30-5.45am Sun-Thu, to 6.45am Fri & Sat; **M** Passeig de Gràcia) One of the top clubs in town for boys seeking boys.

Metro (☎93 323 52 27; www.metrodiscobcn.com; Carrer de Sepúlveda 185; cover before/after 2am from €8/20; ⏰12.15am-5.30am Sun-Thu, to 6.45am Fri & Sat; **M** Universitat) Top-notch DJs preside over two heaving dance floors and other amusements.

Top Tips

- The southern end of Platja de la Mar Bella, located north of Barceloneta, is a gay-male nudist strip from mid-afternoon.
- Find events at 60by80 (www.60by80.com) and Gay Barcelona (www.gaybarcelona.com).

Four Perfect Days

Day 1

CHANTAL DE BRUIJNE/SHUTTERSTOCK ©

Spend your first morning exploring the narrow medieval streets of the Barri Gòtic. Have a peek inside **La Catedral** (p44) and stroll through the picturesque square of **Plaça Reial** (p47). Discover Barcelona's Roman roots in the **Museu d'Història de Barcelona** (p180). Have a wander down La Rambla.

In the afternoon, wander over to La Ribera, which is packed with artistic and architectural treasures, such as the majestic **Basílica de Santa Maria del Mar** (p78) and the **Museu Picasso** (p179).

Before a late dinner, catch a show at the **Palau de la Música Catalana** (p84), one of the great Modernista masterpieces of Barcelona. Afterwards end the night with some funk, soul and a cocktail at lively **Guzzo** (p88).

Day 2

NIKADA/GETTY IMAGES ©

On day two, start with a morning visit to **La Sagrada Família** (p124), Gaudí's wondrous work in progress. It's worth paying a little extra for a guided tour.

After lunch, explore more of the great Modernista buildings by taking a stroll down L'Eixample's Passeig de Gràcia. Visit Gaudí's **Casa Batlló** (p114) or his **La Pedrera** (p108) further up the avenue.

In the evening, catch a football match at **Camp Nou** (p146), home of FC Barcelona. Prepare for a serious adrenaline rush, especially if Barça is playing arch-rival Real Madrid. Afterwards explore lesser-known gems in the area, like the plaza-side **El Maravillas** (p152) (great for tapas and drinks) or **Bangkok Cafe** (p151), serving Barcelona's best Thai dishes.

Day 3

BERNA NAMOGLU/SHUTTERSTOCK ©

On your third day in Barcelona, it's time to take in the lovely Mediterranean. Start the morning with a stroll, jog or bike ride along the waterfront. Beach-facing restaurants and cafes provide refreshment along the way.

Stroll through Barceloneta, stopping for a peek inside the **Mercat de la Barceloneta** (p95). Afterwards visit the **Museu d'Història de Catalunya** (p98) and peel back the centuries on an interactive journey into Catalan history.

At night, catch a live band inside the Gothic quarter. **Harlem Jazz Club** (p56) is a good bet for jazz and world music. If you still have energy, check out bars like **L'Ascensor** (p55), a cosy drinking den with nicely mixed cocktails and a grown-up crowd.

Day 4

STEFANO POLITI MARKOVINA/ALAMY STOCK PHOTO ©

Start the day with a scenic cable-car ride up to Montjuïc, followed by a stroll through gardens to the **Museu Nacional d'Art de Catalunya** (p179). Take in the Romanesque frescoes, Gothic paintings and works by 17th-century Spanish masters.

After getting a taste of Montjuïc, hop on the metro up to Gràcia and wander through its villagey streets. Cafes, bookshops and vintage shops all make for some worthwhile exploring. The bars surrounding its plazas come to life around sundown.

Take in Barcelona's boho side in El Raval. Browse record shops and vintage stores, or watch an indie feature at the **Filmoteca de Catalunya** (p70). Finish the night over tapas and vermouth at **La Confitería** (p68).

Need to Know

For detailed information, see Survival Guide (p174)

Population
1,621,090

Currency
euro (€)

Money
ATMs are widely available (La Rambla has many). Credit cards are accepted in most hotels, shops and restaurants. Major cards are widely accepted.

Languages
Spanish, Catalan

Time
Central European Time (GMT/UTC plus 1 hour)

Visas
No visa required for citizens of EU and Schengen countries. Citizens of other countries should check with their local Spanish embassy.

Mobile Phones
Spain uses GSM 900/1800, compatible with the rest of Europe and Australia but not with the North American GSM 1900 or the system used in Japan.

Daily Budget

Budget: Less than €60

Dorm bed: €17–28

Set lunch: from €11

Bicycle hire per hour: €5

Midrange: €60–200

Standard double room: €80–140

Two-course dinner with wine for two: €50

Walking and guided tours: €15–25

Top end: More than €200

Double room in boutique and luxury hotels: €200 and up

Three-course meal at top restaurants per person: €80

Concert tickets to Palau de la Música Catalana: around €40

Advance Planning

Three months before Book accommodation and reserve a table at a top restaurant.

One month before Check out reviews for theatre and live music, and book tickets.

One week before Browse the latest nightlife listings, art exhibitions and other events to attend while in town. Reserve spa visits and organised tours.

A few days before Check the weather forecast.

Arriving in Barcelona

El Prat Airport

Frequent *aerobúses* make the 35-minute run into town (€5.90) from 6am to 1am. Taxis cost around €26.

Estació Sants

Long-distance trains arrive at this large station near the centre of town, which is linked by metro to other parts of the city.

Estació del Nord

The long-haul bus station is located about 1.5km northeast of Plaça Catalunya, and a short walk from Arc de Triomf metro station.

Girona-Costa Brava Airport

The 'Barcelona Bus' operated by Sagalés (one way/return €16/25, 1½ hours) is timed with Ryanair flights and goes direct to Barcelona's Estació del Nord.

Getting Around

The excellent metro can get you most places, with buses and trams filling in the gaps. The T-10 passes (10 rides; €10.20) are good value.

Metro

Runs 5am to midnight Sunday to Thursday, till 2am on Friday and 24 hours on Saturday.

Bus

Buses run along most city routes every few minutes from around 6am to around 11pm.

Taxi

Yellow and black taxis can be hailed on the street or you can call for one.

Bicycle

Barcelona has over 180km of bike lanes. The city has numerous bike-hire outlets.

KAPUSTIN IGOR/SHUTTERSTOCK ©

Barcelona Neighbourhoods

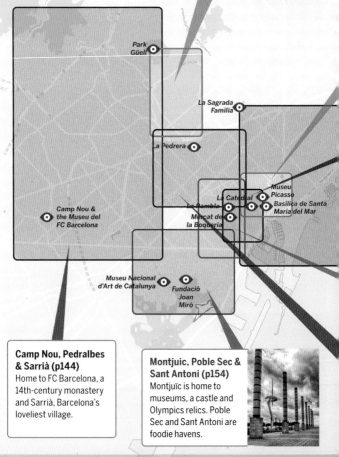

Gràcia & Park Güell (p128)
To the north of laid-back, village-like Gràcia lies one of Gaudí's most captivating works.

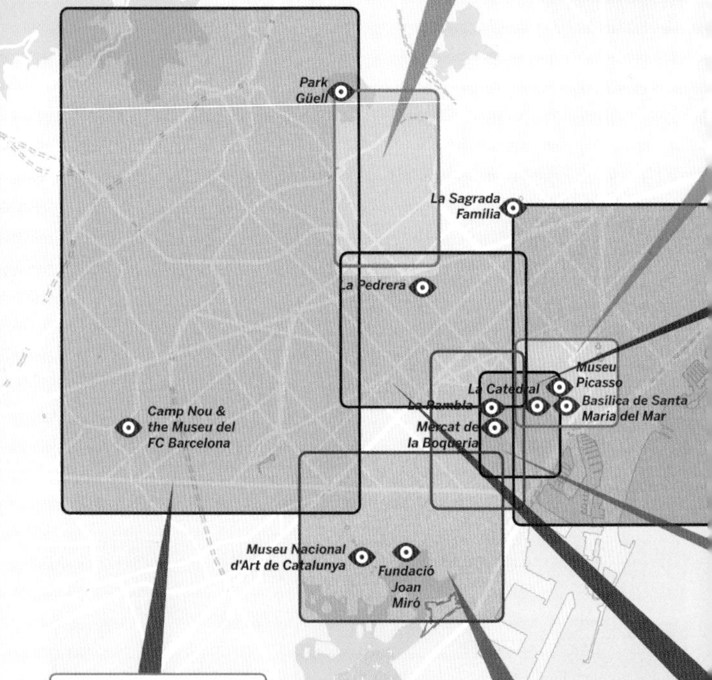

Camp Nou, Pedralbes & Sarrià (p144)
Home to FC Barcelona, a 14th-century monastery and Sarrià, Barcelona's loveliest village.

Montjuïc, Poble Sec & Sant Antoni (p154)
Montjuïc is home to museums, a castle and Olympics relics. Poble Sec and Sant Antoni are foodie havens.

La Ribera & Parc de la Ciutadella (p72)
La Ribera has a wonderful market, splendid architecture, and El Born district – Barcelona's byword for cool.

La Rambla & Barri Gòtic (p38)
Barcelona's old quarter combines famous La Rambla with narrow medieval streets and monumental buildings.

Barceloneta & the Beaches (p92)
Barcelona as it once was with an age-old culture of fishing, and an altogether shinier new beach culture.

El Raval (p58)
The former port district includes a fabulous market, bars and restaurants, stunning art galleries and an unlikely Gaudí confection.

Passeig de Gràcia & L'Eixample (p106)
Explore Modernista treasures, outstanding bars and restaurants, and a shopper's paradise to rival Paris.

Explore Barcelona

City's Walking Tours

A traditional *castell* (human castle) GUILLEM LOPEZ/ALAMY STOCK PHOTO ©

Explore

La Rambla & Barri Gòtic

La Rambla, Barcelona's most famous pedestrian strip, is always a hive of activity, with buskers and peddlers, tourists and con artists (watch out!) mingling amid the crowds gracing the sunlit cafes and shops on the boulevard. The adjoining Barri Gòtic is packed with historical treasures – relics of ancient Rome, 14th-century Gothic churches and atmospheric cobblestone lanes lined with shops, bars and restaurants.

Start your day with an early stroll down La Rambla, then head for La Catedral (p44). Then head next door to the Museu Frederic Marès (p52), punctuated by a coffee in its outdoor cafe.

After a lunch at Cafè de l'Acadèmia (p53), lose yourself in the labyrinth of the old quarter. The city's Roman heritage makes a fine theme on which to focus your meanderings, stopping at the Museu d'Història de Barcelona (p52).

As night falls, after a meal at Belmonte (p54) or Pla (p55), Plaça Reial is a fine place to spend your evening. Catch a show at Jamboree (p56) or Gran Teatre del Liceu (p53).

Getting There

M Key stops near or on La Rambla include Catalunya, Liceu and Drassanes. For Barri Gòtic's east side, Jaume I and Urquinaona are handiest.

Bus: Airport and night buses arrive and depart from Plaça de Catalunya.

Neighbourhood Map on p50

A Barri Gòtic laneway NEJRON PHOTO/SHUTTERSTOCK ©

Top Sight

La Rambla

Barcelona's most famous street is both a tourist magnet and a window into Catalan culture, with cultural centres, theatres and intriguing architecture. The middle of La Rambla is a broad pedestrian boulevard, crowded every day with a wide cross-section of society. A stroll here is pure sensory overload, with souvenir hawkers, buskers, pavement artists, mimes and living statues all part of the ever-changing street scene.

MAP P50, C6

M Catalunya, Liceu, Drassanes

History

La Rambla takes its name from a seasonal stream (*ramla* in Arabic) that once ran here. From the early Middle Ages, it was better known as the Cagalell (Stream of Shit) and lay outside the city walls until the 14th century. Monastic buildings were then built and, subsequently, mansions of the well-to-do from the 16th to the early 19th centuries. Unofficially La Rambla is divided into five sections, which explains why many know it as Las Ramblas.

La Rambla de Canaletes

The section of La Rambla north of Plaça de Catalunya is named after the **Font de Canaletes** (La Rambla; M Catalunya), an inconspicuous turn-of-the-20th-century drinking fountain, the water of which supposedly emerges from what were once known as the springs of Canaletes. It used to be said that a proper *barcelonin* was one who 'drank the waters of Les Canaletes'. Nowadays people claim that anyone who drinks from the fountain will return to Barcelona, which is not such a bad prospect. Delirious football fans gather here to celebrate whenever the main home side, FC Barcelona, wins a cup or the league premiership.

La Rambla dels Estudis

La Rambla dels Estudis, from Carrer de la Canuda running south to Carrer de la Portaferrissa, was formerly home to a twittering bird market, which closed in 2010 after 150 years in operation.

Església de Betlem

Just north of Carrer del Carme, this **church** (93 318 38 23; www.mdbetlem.net; Carrer d'en Xuclà 2; 8.30am-1.30pm & 6-9pm; M Liceu) was constructed in baroque style for the Jesuits in the late 17th and early 18th centuries to replace an earlier church destroyed by fire in 1671. Fire was a bit of a theme for this site: the church was once considered the most splendid of Barcelona's few baroque offerings, but leftist arsonists torched it in 1936.

★ Top Tips

- La Rambla is at its best first thing in the morning, before the cruise ships disgorge their passengers.
- Do keep an eye on your belongings and wear backpacks on your front. Pickpockets find easy pickings along this stretch.

Take a Break

For a proper sit-down meal, your best nearby bet is at one of the many restaurants ringing the Plaça Reial (p47).

The best spot for breakfast – or coffee at any time of day – is the **Café de l'Opera** (93 317 75 85; www.cafeoperabcn.com; La Rambla 74; 8am-2am; ; M Liceu).

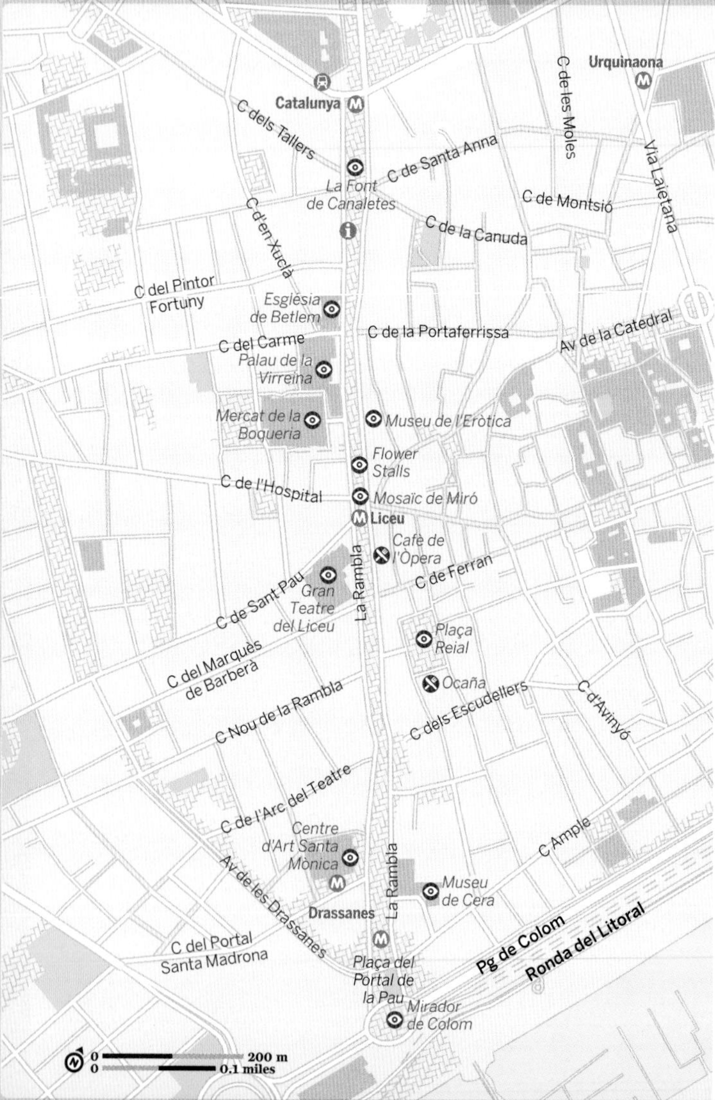
Catalunya
Urquinaona
C dels Tallers
C de les Moles
Via Laietana
C de Santa Anna
La Font de Canaletes
C de Montsió
C d'en Xuclà
C de la Canuda
C del Pintor Fortuny
Esglèsia de Betlem
C de la Portaferrissa
Av de la Catedral
C del Carme
Palau de la Virreina
Mercat de la Boqueria
Museu de l'Eròtica
Flower Stalls
C de l'Hospital
Mosaïc de Miró
Liceu
Cafè de l'Òpera
C de Ferran
C de Sant Pau
Gran Teatre del Liceu
La Rambla
Plaça Reial
C del Marquès de Barberà
Ocaña
C Nou de la Rambla
C dels Escudellers
C d'Avinyó
C de l'Arc del Teatre
Centre d'Art Santa Mònica
C Ample
Av de les Drassanes
Museu de Cera
Drassanes
La Rambla
C del Portal Santa Madrona
Pg de Colom
Ronda del Litoral
Plaça del Portal de la Pau
Mirador de Colom
0 200 m
0 0.1 miles

Palau Moja

Looming over the eastern side of La Rambla, **Palau Moja** (93 316 27 40; https://palaumoja.com; Carrer de Portaferrissa 1; admission free; 10am-9pm, cafe 9.30am-midnight Mon-Fri, 11am-midnight Sat & Sun; M Liceu) is a neoclassical building dating from the second half of the 18th century. Its clean, classical lines are best appreciated from across the other side of the street. It mostly houses government offices, but access is now an option thanks to a large gift shop and cafe.

La Rambla de Sant Josep

From Carrer de la Portaferrissa to Plaça de la Boqueria, what is officially called La Rambla de Sant Josep (named after a now nonexistent monastery) is lined with flower stalls, which give it the alternative name La Rambla de les Flors. This stretch also contains the bawdy **Museu de l'Eròtica** (Erotica Museum; 93 318 98 65; www.erotica-museum.com; La Rambla 96; €10; 10am-midnight; M Liceu).

Palau de la Virreina

This grand 18th-century rococo (with some neoclassical elements) **mansion** (La Rambla 99; M Liceu) now houses the **Centre de la Imatge** (93 316 10 00; www.ajuntament.barcelona.cat/lavirreina; admission free; noon-8pm Tue-Sun), which has rotating photography exhibits.

Just south of the Palau, in El Raval, is the Mercat de la Boqueria (p60), one of the best-stocked and most colourful produce markets in Europe.

Mosaïc de Miró

At Plaça de la Boqueria, where four side streets meet just north of Liceu metro station, you can walk all over a Miró – the colourful **mosaic** in the pavement, with one tile signed by the artist. Miró chose this site as it's near the house where he was born on the Passatge del Crèdit. The mosaic's bold colours and vivid swirling forms are instantly recognisable to Miró fans, though plenty of tourists stroll right over it without realising.

La Rambla dels Caputxins

La Rambla dels Caputxins, named after a former monastery, runs from Plaça de la Boqueria to Carrer dels Escudellers. The latter street is named after the potters' guild, founded in the 13th century, the members of which lived and worked here. On the western side of La Rambla is the Gran Teatre del Liceu (p53); to the southeast is the entrance to the palm-shaded Plaça Reial (p47). Below this point La Rambla gets seedier.

La Rambla de Santa Mónica

The final stretch of La Rambla widens out to approach the Mirador de Colom (p99) overlooking Port Vell. La Rambla here is named after the Convent de Santa Mònica, which once stood on the western flank of the street and has since been converted into the **Centre d'Art Santa Mònica** (93 567 11 10; http://artssantamonica.gencat.cat; La Rambla 7; admission free; 11am-9pm Tue-Sat, 11am-5pm Sun; M Drassanes), a cultural centre that mostly exhibits modern multimedia installations.

Top Sight

La Catedral

Barcelona's central place of worship presents a magnificent image. The richly decorated main facade, laced with gargoyles and the stone intricacies you would expect of northern European Gothic, sets it quite apart from other churches in Barcelona. The facade was actually added in 1870, although the rest of the building was built between 1298 and 1460.

MAP P50, D3

www.catedralbcn.org

Plaça de la Seu

donation entrance €7, choir €3, roof €3

8am-12.45pm & 5.45-7.30pm Mon-Fri, 8am-8pm Sat & Sun, entry by donation 1-5.30pm Mon,1-5pm Sat, 2-5pm Sun

M Jaume I

The Interior

The interior is a broad, soaring space divided into a central nave and two aisles by lines of elegant, slim pillars. The cathedral was one of the few churches in Barcelona spared by the anarchists in the civil war, so its ornamentation, never overly lavish, is intact.

The Roof

For a bird's-eye view (mind the poo) of medieval Barcelona, visit the cathedral's roof and tower by taking the lift (€3) from the Capella de les Animes del Purgatori near the northeast transept.

Claustre

From the southwest transept, exit by the partly Romanesque door (one of the few remnants of the present church's predecessor) to the leafy *claustre* (cloister), with its fountains and flock of 13 geese. The geese supposedly represent the age of Santa Eulàlia at the time of her martyrdom and have, generation after generation, been squawking here since medieval days. One of the cloister chapels commemorates 930 priests, monks and nuns martyred during the civil war.

In the northwest corner of the cloister is the **Capella de Santa Llúcia** (Plaça de la Seu; admission free; 8am-7.30pm Mon-Fri, to 8pm Sat & Sun; M Jaume I), one of the few reminders of Romanesque Barcelona (although the interior is largely Gothic).

★ Top Tips

- It is worth paying for the 'donation entrance' to avoid the crowds and appreciate the splendour of the building in relative peace.
- If you're around at 6pm on Saturday or 11am on Sunday, check out the *sardanes* (the Catalan national dance) in the square in front of the cathedral.

Take a Break

Head to the Carrer dels Banys Nous for a fortifying cone of churros – deep-fried batter sticks – at **Xurreria** (93 318 76 91; Carrer dels Banys Nous 8; cone €1.20; 7am-1.30pm & 3.30-8.15pm Mon-Fri, 7am-2pm & 3.30-8.30pm Sat & Sun; M Jaume I).

A couple of minutes' walk away, **Els Quatre Gats** (93 302 41 40; www.4gats.com; Carrer de Montsió 3; mains €23-29; 1-4pm & 7pm-1am; M Urquinaona) makes for an architecturally splendid pit stop.

Walking Tour

Hidden Treasures in the Barri Gòtic

This scenic walk through the Barri Gòtic will take you back in time, right from the early days of Roman-era Barcino through to the medieval era. The 20th century has also left its mark on the area, from artistic contributions to the tragic scars of the Spanish Civil War.

Walk Facts

Start Col•legi de Arquitectes

End Plaça del Rei

Length 1.5km; 1½ hours

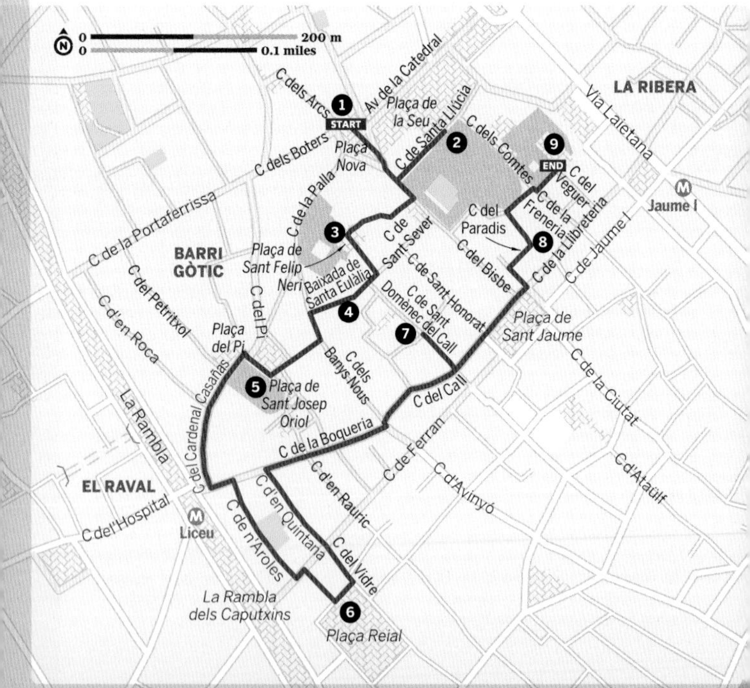

❶ Picasso friezes

Before entering the cathedral, have a look at the child-like scribblings on facade of the **Col•legi de Arquitectes** building facing the Plaça Nova. It is, in fact, a giant contribution by Picasso from 1962, representing Mediterranean festivals.

❷ La Catedral

After noting his signature style, wander through **La Catedral** (p44); don't miss the cloister with its flock of 13 geese.

❸ Plaça de Sant Felip Neri

Leaving the cathedral, enter the former gates of the ancient fortified city and turn right into **Plaça de Sant Felip Neri**. Note the shrapnel-scarred walls of the old church, damaged by pro-Francoist bombers in 1938. A plaque commemorates the victims (mostly children) of the bombing.

❹ Santa Eulàlia

Head out of the square and turn right. On this narrow lane, you'll spot a small **statue of Santa Eulàlia**, one of Barcelona's patron saints who suffered various tortures during her martyrdom.

❺ Basílica de Santa Maria del Pi

Make your way west to the looming 14th-century **Basílica de Santa Maria del Pi** (☎93 318 47 43; www.basilicadelpi.com; Plaça del Pi; adult/concession/child under 7yr €4/3/free; ⌚10am-6pm; Ⓜ Liceu), which is famed for its magnificent rose window.

❻ Plaça Reial

Follow the curving road and zigzag down to **Plaça Reial**, one of Barcelona's prettiest squares. Flanking the fountain are lamp posts designed by Antoni Gaudí.

❼ Sinagoga Major

Stroll up to Carrer de la Boqueria and turn left on Carrer de Sant Domènec del Call. This leads into the El Call district, once the heart of the medieval Jewish quarter, until the bloody pogrom of 1391. The **Sinagoga Major** (☎93 317 07 90; www.calldebarcelona.org; Carrer de Marlet 5; adult/child under 11yr €2.50/free; ⌚10.30am-6.30pm Mon-Fri, to 2.30pm Sat & Sun Apr-Sep, 11am-5.30pm Mon-Fri, to 3pm Sat & Sun Oct-Mar; Ⓜ Liceu), one of Europe's oldest, was discovered in 1996.

❽ Roman Temple

Head across Plaça de Sant Jaume and turn left after Carrer del Bisbe. You'll soon pass the entrance to the remnants of a **Roman temple**, with four columns hidden in a small courtyard.

❾ Plaça del Rei

The final stop is **Plaça del Rei**, a picturesque plaza where Fernando and Isabel received Columbus following his first New World voyage. The former palace today houses a superb history museum (p52), with significant Roman ruins underground.

Walking Tour

A Barri Gòtic Sunday Walk

The Barri Gòtic can seem overrun by visitors at times, but it's on Sunday more than any other day that locals reclaim their neighbourhood, colonising the squares with small markets and frequenting places little known to out-of-town visitors. Sunday is also the only day when the town hall – a Catalan icon – throws open its doors.

Walk Facts

Start Església de Sants Just i Pastor

End Granja la Pallaresa

Length 1.6km; all day

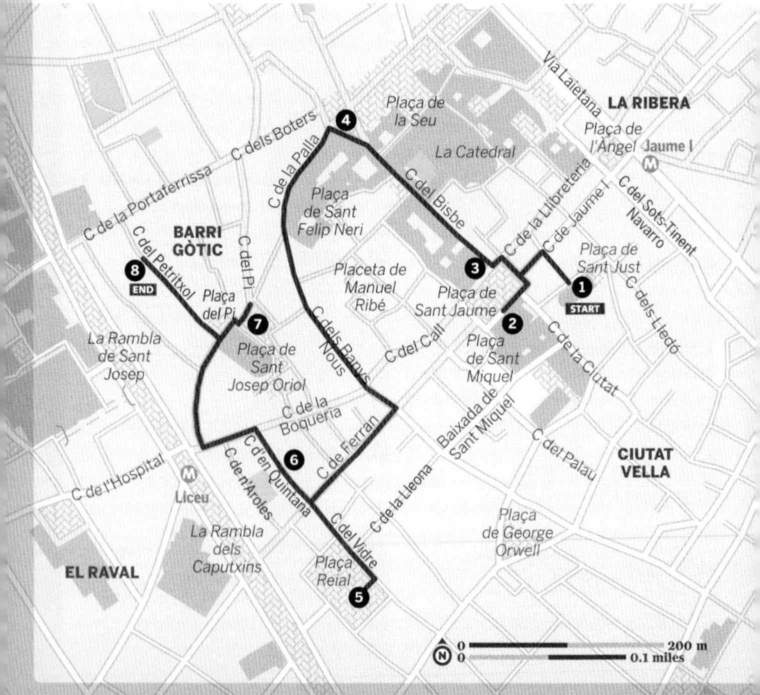

❶ Spiritual Start

Sunday mass remains an important part of life in the Barri Gòtic, so where better to begin than the 14th-century **Església de Sants Just i Pastor** (www.basilicasantjust.cat; 11am-2pm & 5-9pm Mon & Wed-Sat, to 8pm Tue, 10am-1pm Sun)? This Gothic church holds a special place in Catalan hearts: on 11 September 1924, Gaudí was arrested here for refusing to speak Spanish to a policeman.

❷ Town Hall Tour

Barcelona's **Ajuntament** (www.bcn.cat; 10.30am-1.30pm Sun;) has been the seat of city power since the 14th century. It has a Catalan Gothic side facade, while its spectacular interior features a majestic staircase and the splendidly restored Saló de Cent (Chamber of the One Hundred).

❸ Catalan Power

The **Palau de la Generalitat** (http://presidencia.gencat.cat; 2nd & 4th weekend of month), the seat of Catalonia's regional government, was adapted from several Gothic mansions. The Saló de Sant Jordi (Hall of St George) is typical of the sumptuous interior. Visits must be booked online.

❹ Sardana

Catching a performance of *sardana,* the Catalan folk dance par excellence, is always a memorable event, at once an enjoyable spectacle and an important reassertion of Catalan identity. Your best chance is to turn up to **Plaça Nova**, next to La Catedral, at 11am on Sundays (or 6pm on Saturdays), when performances usually take place.

❺ Coins & Stamps

While much of Barcelona is still sleeping off the excesses of the night before, dedicated collectors make their way to the **Coin & Stamp Market** (9am-2.30pm Sun). Like all flea markets, it's always worth leafing through what's on offer in search of treasure, while some stallholders have branched out to sell a range of knick-knacks, both antique and otherwise.

❻ Sunday Lunch

Founded in 1786, **Can Culleretes** (p54) is still going strong, with crowds flocking to enjoy its rambling interior, old-fashioned tile-filled decor, and enormous helpings of traditional Catalan food.

❼ Art & Crafts Market

On one of the Barri Gòtic's prettiest little squares, you'll find dozens of local artists and artisans showcasing their work in this lively **crafts market** (11am-8pm Sat, to 2pm Sun). It happens on Plaça de Sant Josep Oriol, which is named after the 17th-century parish priest (canonised in 1909) based in the church here.

❽ Chocolate con Churros

An afternoon favourite for barcelonins, **Granja La Pallaresa** (www.lapallaresa.com; Carrer del Petritxol 11; 9am-1pm & 4-9pm Mon-Sat, 9am-1pm & 5-9pm Sun) serves up thick and rich hot chocolate. Order some crispy churros (*xurros* in Catalan; deep-fried dough strips) for some delectable dunking.

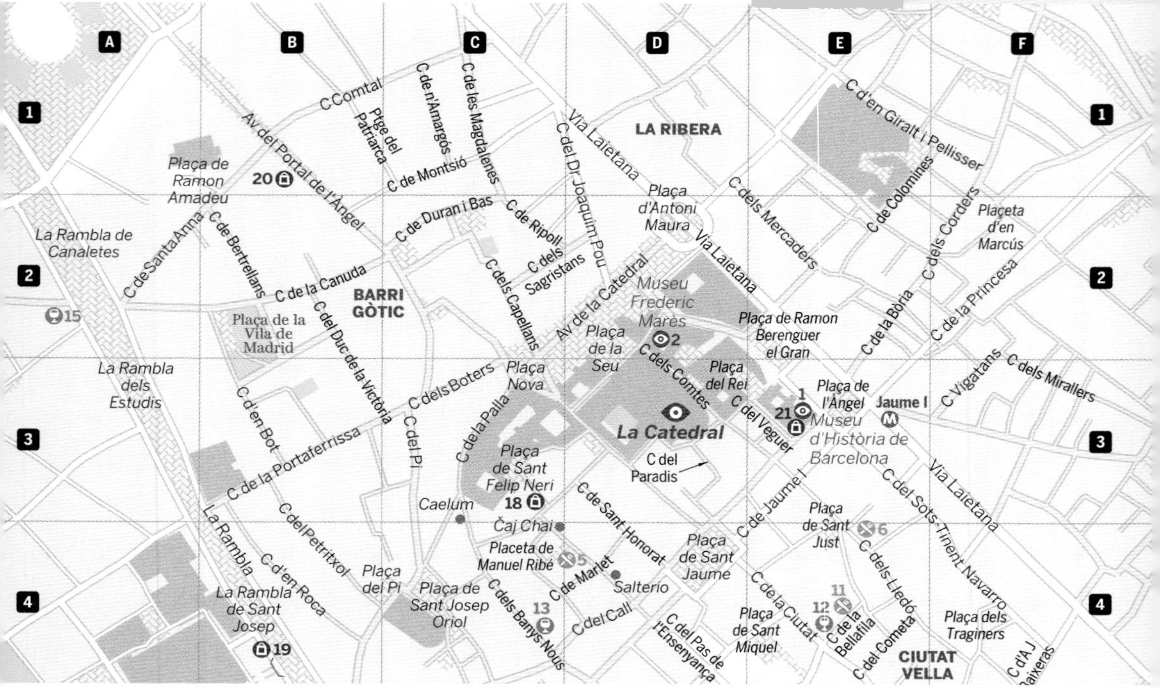
A
B
C
D
E
F
1
2
3
4
LA RIBERA
BARRI GÒTIC
CIUTAT VELLA
La Catedral
C Comtal
Ptge del Patriarca
C de n'Amargós
C de les Magdalenes
C de Montsió
Av del Portal de l'Àngel
Plaça de Ramon Amadeu
20
C de Duran i Bas
C de Ripoll
C del Dr Joaquim Pou
Via Laietana
Plaça d'Antoni Maura
C dels Mercaders
C d'en Giralt i Pellisser
C de Colomines
C dels Corders
Placeta d'en Marcús
C de la Princesa
C de la Bòria
C Vigatans
C dels Mirallers
La Rambla de Canaletes
C de Santa Anna
C de Bertrellans
C de la Canuda
C dels Sagristans
C dels Capellans
Av de la Catedral
Museu Frederic Marès
2
Plaça de Ramon Berenguer el Gran
15
Plaça de la Vila de Madrid
C del Duc de la Victòria
Plaça de la Seu
C dels Comtes
Plaça del Rei
C del Veguer
Plaça de l'Àngel
1
21
Jaume I
Museu d'Història de Barcelona
La Rambla dels Estudis
C d'en Bot
C dels Boters
Plaça Nova
C de la Palla
C del Pi
C de la Portaferrissa
Plaça de Sant Felip Neri
18
C del Paradis
C de Jaume I
C del Sots-Tinent Navarro
Caelum
Čaj Chai
C de Sant Honorat
Plaça de Sant Just
6
La Rambla
C del Petritxol
Placeta de Manuel Ribé
5
Plaça de Sant Jaume
C d'en Roca
Plaça del Pi
Plaça de Sant Josep Oriol
C de Marlet
Salterio
C dels Lledó
C dels Banys Nous
13
C del Call
C de la Ciutat
11
12
Plaça dels Traginers
La Rambla de Sant Josep
19
C del Pas de l'Ensenyança
Plaça de Sant Miquel
C de la Bellafila
C del Cometa
C d'A J Baixeras

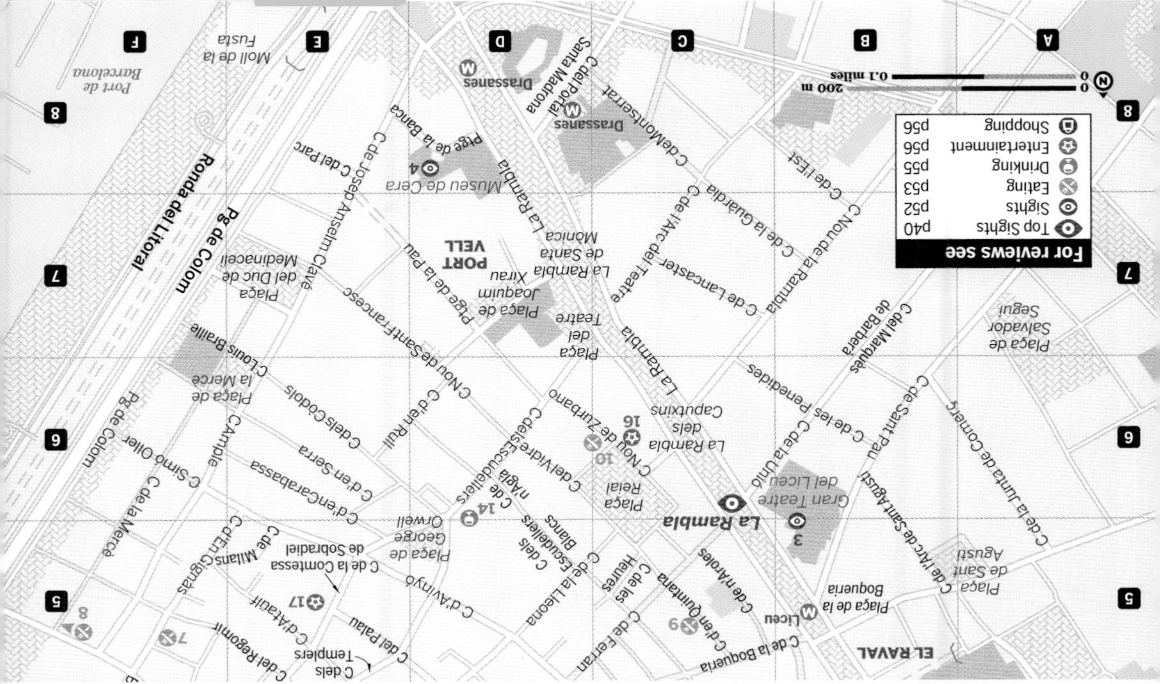
For reviews see
Top Sights p40
Sights p52
Eating p53
Drinking p55
Entertainment p56
Shopping p56
0 200 m
0 0.1 miles
EL RAVAL
PORT VELL
La Rambla
Gran Teatre del Liceu
Plaça de la Boqueria
Plaça de Sant Agustí
Plaça de Salvador Seguí
Plaça Reial
Plaça del Teatre
Plaça de Joaquim Xirau
Plaça de George Orwell
Plaça de la Mercè
Plaça del Duc de Medinaceli
La Rambla dels Caputxins
La Rambla de Santa Mònica
Museu de Cera
Drassanes
Liceu
Port de Barcelona
Moll de la Fusta
Ronda del Litoral
Pg de Colom
C de la Boqueria
C d'en Quintana
C de n'Aroles
C de Ferran
C de les Heures
C de la Lleona
C dels Escudellers Blancs
C de n'Aglà
C dels Escudellers
C del Vidre
C Nou de Zurbano
C d'Avinyó
C del Palau
C dels Templers
C del Regomir
C d'Ataülf
C de la Comtessa de Sobradiel
C de Milans
C d'En Gignàs
C de la Mercè
C Simó Oller
C Ample
C d'en Carabassa
C d'en Serra
C dels Còdols
C Louis Braille
C d'en Rull
C Nou de Sant Francesc
Ptge de la Pau
C de Josep Anselm Clavé
C del Parc
Ptge de la Banca
C del Portal Santa Madrona
C de Montserrat
C de l'Arc del Teatre
C de Lancaster
C de la Guàrdia
C Nou de la Rambla
C de l'Est
C del Marquès de Barberà
C de les Penedides
C de la Unió
C de Sant Pau
C de l'Arc de Sant Agustí
C de la Junta de Comerç

Sights

Museu d'Història de Barcelona MUSEUM

1 MAP P50, E3

One of Barcelona's most fascinating museums takes you back through the centuries to the very foundations of Roman Barcino. You'll stroll over ruins of the old streets, sewers, laundries and wine- and fish-making factories that flourished here following the town's founding by Emperor Augustus around 10 BC. Equally impressive is the building itself, which was once part of the Palau Reial Major (Grand Royal Palace) on Plaça del Rei, among the key locations of medieval princely power in Barcelona. (MUHBA; 93 256 21 00; www.museuhistoria.bcn.cat; Plaça del Rei; adult/concession/child €7/5/free, 3-8pm Sun & 1st Sun of month free; 10am-7pm Tue-Sat, to 2pm Mon, to 8pm Sun; M Jaume I)

Museu Frederic Marès MUSEUM

2 MAP P50, D2

One of the wildest collections of historical curios lies inside this vast medieval complex, once part of the royal palace of the counts of Barcelona. A rather worn coat of arms on the wall indicates that it was also, for a while, the seat of the Spanish Inquisition in Barcelona. Frederic Marès i Deulovol (1893–1991) was a rich sculptor, traveller and obsessive collector, and displays of religious art and vast varieties of antiques *objets* litter the museum. (93 256 35

Statues at Museu Frederic Marès

GUY MOBERLY/LONELY PLANET ©

00; www.museumares.bcn.cat; Plaça de Sant Iu 5; adult/concession/child €4.20/2.40/free, 3-8pm Sun & 1st Sun of month free; 10am-7pm Tue-Sat, 11am-8pm Sun; M Jaume I)

Gran Teatre del Liceu ARCHITECTURE

3 MAP P50, B5

If you can't catch a night at the opera, you can still have a look around one of Europe's greatest opera houses, known to locals as the Liceu. Smaller than Milan's La Scala but bigger than Venice's La Fenice, it can seat up to 2300 people in its grand auditorium. (93 485 99 00; www.liceubarcelona.cat; La Rambla 51-59; tours adult/concession/child under 7yr 45min €9/7.50/free, 25min €6/5/free; 45min tours hourly 2-6pm Mon-Fri, from 9.30am Sat, 25min tours 1.30pm Mon-Sat; M Liceu)

Museu de Cera MUSEUM

4 MAP P50, D8

Inside this late-19th-century building you can wander about looking at Frankenstein, Che Guevara, Lady Diana and lots of Spanish figures you probably won't recognise. It's unintentionally funny, with a price tag that's steep for often poorly executed representations, although small children are generally enthusiastic. (93 317 26 49; www.museocerabcn.com; Passatge de la Banca 7; adult/concession/child under 5yr €15/9/free; 10am-10pm Jul-Sep, 10am-1.30pm & 4-7.30pm Mon-Fri, 11am-2pm & 4.30-8.30pm Sat & Sun Oct-Jun; M Drassanes)

Eating

La Vinateria del Call SPANISH €€

5 MAP P50, D4

In a magical setting in the former Jewish quarter, this tiny jewel-box of a restaurant serves up tasty Iberian dishes including Galician octopus, cider-cooked chorizo and the Catalan *escalivada* (roasted peppers, aubergine and onions) with anchovies. Portions are small and made for sharing, and there's a good and affordable selection of wines. (93 302 60 92; www.lavinateriadelcall.com; Carrer de Sant Domènec del Call 9; raciones €7-12; 7.30pm-1am; ; M Jaume I)

Cafè de l'Acadèmia CATALAN €€

6 MAP P50, E4

Expect a mix of traditional Catalan dishes with the occasional creative twist. At lunchtime, local city hall workers pounce on the *menú del día* (€15.75). In the evening it is rather more romantic, as low lighting emphasises the intimacy of the beamed ceiling and stone walls. On warm days you can also dine in the pretty square at the front. (93 319 82 53; Carrer dels Lledó 1; mains €15-20; 1-3.30pm & 8-11pm Mon-Fri; ; M Jaume I)

Milk INTERNATIONAL €

7 MAP P50, F5

Also known to many as an enticing cocktail spot, Irish-run Milk's key role for Barcelona night owls is providing morning-after brunches (served till 4.30pm). Avoid direct sunlight and tuck into pancakes, eggs Benedict and other hangover dishes in a cosy lounge-like setting complete with ornate wallpaper, framed prints on the wall and cushion-lined seating. The musical selection is also notable. (93 268 09 22; www.milkbarcelona.com; Carrer d'en Gignàs 21; mains €9-12; 9am-2am Thu-Mon, to 3am Fri & Sat; ; Jaume I)

Belmonte TAPAS €€

8 MAP P50, F5

This tiny tapas joint in the southern reaches of Barri Gòtic whips up beautifully prepared small plates – including an excellent *truita* (tortilla), rich *patatons a la sal* (salted new potatoes with *romesco* sauce) and tender *carpaccio de pop* (octopus carpaccio). Wash it down with the homemade *vermut* (vermouth). (93 310 76 84; Carrer de la Mercè 29; tapas €4-10, mains €13-14; 8pm-midnight Tue-Fri, 1-3.30pm & 8pm-midnight Sat Jul-Oct, 7.30pm-midnight Tue-Thu, 1-3.30pm & 7.30pm-midnight Fri & Sat Oct-Jun; ; Jaume I)

Can Culleretes CATALAN €€

9 MAP P50, C5

Founded in 1786, Barcelona's oldest restaurant is still going strong, with tourists and locals flocking here to enjoy its rambling interior, old-fashioned tile-filled decor and enormous helpings of traditional Catalan food, including fresh seafood and sticky stews. From Tuesday to Friday there is a fixed lunch menu for €14.50. (93 317 30 22; www.culleretes.com; Carrer d'en Quintana 5; mains €10-18; 1.30-3.45pm & 8-10.45pm Tue-Sat, 1.30-3.45pm Sun; ; Liceu)

Ocaña INTERNATIONAL €€

10 MAP P50, C6

A flamboyant but elegantly designed space of high ceilings,

El Call

El Call (pronounced 'kye', and which probably derives from the Hebrew word kahal, meaning 'community') is the name of the medieval Jewish quarter that flourished here until a tragic pogrom in the 14th century. It is a tiny area, and a little tricky to find. The boundaries are roughly Carrer del Call, Carrer dels Banys Nous, Baixada de Santa Eulàlia and Carrer de Sant Honorat.

Though a handful of Jewish families remained after the bloody pogrom of 1391, the subsequent expulsion of all Jews in the country in the 15th century put an end to the Jewish presence in Barcelona. The Call Menor extended across the modern Carrer de Ferran as far as Baixada de Sant Miquel and Carrer d'en Rauric. The present Església de Sant Jaume on Carrer de Ferran was built on the site of a synagogue.

Even before the pogrom, Jews in Barcelona were not privileged citizens. As in many medieval centres, they were obliged to wear a special identifying mark on their garments and had trouble getting permission to expand their ghetto as El Call's population increased (as many as 4000 people were crammed into the tiny streets of the Call Major).

chandeliers and plush furnishings, Ocaña blends late-night carousing with serious eating. The Spanish and Catalan dishes are given a creative and successful twist, and are now complemented on Thursday, Friday and Saturday nights by a superb selection of Mexican dishes. (93 676 48 14; www.ocana.cat; Plaça Reial 13; mains €9.50-16; noon-2am Sun-Thu, to 2.30am Fri & Sat; ; Liceu)

Pla

FUSION €€

11 MAP P50, E4

One of Gòtic's long-standing favourites, Pla is a stylish, romantically lit medieval dining room where the cooks churn out such temptations as oxtail braised in red wine, seared tuna with oven-roasted peppers, and polenta with seasonal mushrooms. (93 412 65 52; www.restaurantpla.cat; Carrer de la Bellafila 5; mains €17-23; 1.30-5.30pm & 7-11.30pm Sun-Thu, to midnight Fri & Sat; ; Jaume I)

Drinking

L'Ascensor

COCKTAIL BAR

12 MAP P50, E4

Named after the lift (elevator) doors that serve as the front door, this elegant drinking den with its vaulted brick ceilings, vintage mirrors and marble-topped bar gathers a faithful crowd that comes for old-fashioned cocktails and lively conversation against a soundtrack of up-tempo jazz and funk. (93 318 53 47; Carrer de la Bellafila 3; 6pm-2.30am Mon-Thu, to 3am Fri-Sun; ; Jaume I)

La Granja

CAFE

13 MAP P50, C4

This long-running cafe serves up thick, rich cups of chocolate, in varying formats, but it doesn't make its own churros. Buy them a few doors down at Xurreria (p45) and bring them here for the perfect combo of churros dipped in chocolate. Also worth a look is the section of Roman wall visible at the back. (93 302 69 75; Carrer dels Banys Nous 4; 9am-9pm; ; Jaume I)

Marula Café

BAR

14 MAP P50, D6

A fantastic find in the heart of the Barri Gòtic, Marula will transport you to the 1970s and the best in funk and soul. James Brown fans will think they've died and gone to heaven. It's not, however, a monothematic place: DJs slip in other tunes, from breakbeat to house. Samba and other Brazilian dance sounds also penetrate here. (93 318 76 90; www.marulacafe.com; Carrer dels Escudellers 49; cover up to €10; 11pm-5am Mon-Thu & Sun, 11.30pm-6am Fri, 9.30pm-6am Sat; Liceu)

Boadas

COCKTAIL BAR

15 MAP P50, A2

One of the city's oldest cocktail bars, Boadas is famed for its daiquiris. Bow-tied waiters have been serving up unique, drinkable creations since Miguel Boadas opened it in 1933 – in fact Miró and Hemingway both drank here. Miguel was born in Havana, where

Barri Gòtic Cafes

Some of Barcelona's most atmospheric cafes lie hidden in the old cobbled lanes of the Barri Gòtic. **Salterio** (Map p50, D4; 93 302 50 28; Carrer de Sant Domènec del Call 4; noon-1am; ; Jaume I) serves teas and sardo (grilled flatbread pizzas) amid stone walls and ambient Middle Eastern music. Nearby, **Čaj Chai** (Map p50, C4; 93 301 95 92; www.cajchai.com; Carrer de Sant Domènec del Call 12; 10.30am-10pm; Jaume I) is a bright and buzzing tearoom with numerous teas on offer. Famed for its heavenly desserts, **Caelum** (Map p50, C3; 93 302 69 93; Carrer de la Palla 8; 10am-8.30pm Mon-Fri, to 9pm Sat & Sun; ; Liceu) has a dainty upstairs cafe as well as an underground chamber with medieval stone walls and flickering candles.

he was the first barman at the immortal La Floridita. (93 318 95 92; www.boadascocktails.com; Carrer dels Tallers 1; noon-2am Mon-Thu, to 3am Fri & Sat; Catalunya)

Entertainment

Jamboree LIVE MUSIC

16 MAP P50, C6

For over half a century, Jamboree has been bringing joy to the jivers of Barcelona, with high-calibre acts featuring jazz trios, blues, Afrobeats, Latin and big-band sounds. Two concerts are held most nights (at 8pm and 10pm), after which Jamboree morphs into a DJ-spinning club at midnight. WTF jam sessions are held Mondays (entrance a mere €5). (93 319 17 89; www.masimas.com/jamboree; Plaça Reial 17; tickets €5-20; 8pm-6am; Liceu)

Harlem Jazz Club JAZZ

17 MAP P50, E5

This narrow, old-city dive is one of the best spots in town for jazz, as well as funk, Latin, blues and gypsy jazz. It attracts a mixed crowd that maintains a respectful silence during the acts. Most concerts start around 10pm. Get in early if you want a seat in front of the stage. (93 310 07 55; www.harlemjazzclub.es; Carrer de la Comtessa de Sobradiel 8; tickets €7-10; 8pm-3am Sun & Tue-Thu, to 5am Fri & Sat; Liceu)

Shopping

Sabater Hermanos COSMETICS

18 MAP P50, C3

This fragrant little shop sells handcrafted soaps of all sizes. Varieties such as fig, cinnamon, grapefruit and chocolate smell good enough to eat, while sandalwood, magnolia, mint, cedar and jasmine add spice to any sink or bathtub. (93 301 98 32; www.sabaterhermanos.es; Plaça de Sant Felip Neri 1; 10.30am-9pm; Jaume I)

Escribà

FOOD & DRINKS

19 MAP P50, B4

Chocolates, dainty pastries and mouth-watering cakes can be nibbled behind the Modernista mosaic facade here or taken away for private, guilt-ridden consumption. This Barcelona favourite is owned by the Escribà family, a name synonymous with sinfully good sweet things. More than that, it adds a touch of authenticity to La Rambla. (93 301 60 27; www.escriba.es; La Rambla 83; 9am-9.30pm; ; M Liceu)

El Corte Inglés

DEPARTMENT STORE

20 MAP P50, B1

A secondary branch of Spain's only remaining department store, selling electronics, fashion, stationery and sports gear. (93 306 38 00; www.elcorteingles.es; Av del Portal de l'Àngel 19-21; 9.30am-9pm Mon-Sat Oct-May, 9.30am-10.15pm Jun-Sep; M Catalunya)

Cereria Subirà

HOMEWARES

21 MAP P50, E3

Even if you're not interested in myriad mounds of colourful wax, pop in just so you've been to the oldest shop in Barcelona. Cereria Subirà has been churning out candles since 1761 and at this address since the 19th century; the interior has a beautifully baroque quality, with a picturesque *Gone With the Wind*–style staircase. (93 315 26 06; http://cereriasubira.net; Calle de la Llibreteria 7; 9.30am-1.30pm & 4-8pm Mon-Thu, 9.30am-8pm Fri, 10am-8pm Sat; M Jaume I)

Café de L'Opera (p41)

Explore El Raval

The once down-and-out district of El Raval is still seedy in parts, though it has seen remarkable rejuvenation in recent years, with the addition of cutting-edge museums and cultural centres, including the Richard Meier-designed Museu d'Art Contemporani de Barcelona (p65).

The Mercat de la Boqueria (p60) ranks among the most enduring of Barcelona institutions and it's at its best in the morning. Leave behind the cries of fishmongers and make your way to the MACBA to sample the cutting edge of contemporary art.

After a lunch in stylish surroundings at Gats (p67), take in an exhibition or two at the Centre de Cultura Contemporània de Barcelona (p66).

Head south via Barcelona's favourite milk bar, Granja M Viader (p69), to the old city's only Gaudí masterpiece, Palau Güell (p65), then continue on to Església de Sant Pau del Camp (p66), one of Barcelona's most tranquil churches.

Start off the evening with a show at Jazz Sí Club (p70), followed by dinner at celebrated Suculent (p68). Afterwards take in El Raval's nightlife at vintage drinking spots like Bar Marsella (p69) or La Confitería (p68).

Getting There

M El Raval is encircled by three metro lines. Línies 1, 2 and 3 stop at strategic points around the district, so nothing is far from a metro stop. The Línia 3 stop at Liceu is a convenient exit point.

Neighbourhood Map on p64

Palau Güell (p65) FRANKII/SHUTTERSTOCK ©

Top Sight

Mercat de la Boqueria

Barcelona's most central produce market, the Mercat de la Boqueria, provides one of the greatest sound, smell and colour sensations in Europe, and is housed in a building every bit as impressive. It spills over with the rich and varied colours of plentiful fruit and vegetable stands, and seemingly limitless varieties of sea critters, cheeses and meats.

MAP P64, C3

93 318 20 17

www.boqueria.info

La Rambla 91

8am-8.30pm Mon-Sat

M Liceu

History

It is believed that there has been a market in this location since 1217, and, as much as it has become a modern-day attraction, it has always been the place where locals have come to shop. What is now known as La Boqueria didn't come to exist until the 19th century, and the iron Modernista gate was constructed in 1914.

Specialities

La Boqueria has a handful of unassuming places to eat – and eat well – although many of them open only at lunchtime. It's worth picking up some of Catalonia's gastronomic specialities, such as *bacallà salat* (dried salt cod), *calçots* (spring onions) when in season, *cargols* (snails), *peus de porc* (pig's trotters) and *percebes* (goose-necked barnacles).

Many of Barcelona's top restaurateurs buy their produce here, although nowadays it's no easy task getting past the seething crowds of tourists to snare a slippery slab of sole or tempting piece of goat's cheese.

Fish Market

While stalls aimed at tourists make tentative inroads, the fish market in La Boqueria's geographical centre is the guardian of tradition. Razor clams and red prawns, salmon, sea bass and swordfish, all almost as fresh as when it was caught; so much so that there's scarcely a fishy aroma to inhale. Barcelona's love affair with fish and seafood starts here.

★ Top Tips

- The market is closed on Sunday.
- Many stalls, including most of those selling fish, are closed on Monday.
- The market's stallholders are among the world's most photographed – ask permission before taking pictures and where possible buy something from their stall.
- Gather food from your favourite stalls with a picnic in mind – having a foodie purpose brings a whole new dimension to your market experience.
- Avoid the stalls at the front, which cater mostly to tourists, and head into the labyrinth.

Take a Break

For market-fresh food and some of the market's best cooking, pull up a stool at **El Quim** (93 301 98 10; www.elquimdelaboqueria.com; Mercat de la Boqueria; mains €16-21; noon-4pm Mon, 7am-4pm Tue-Thu, 7am-5pm Fri & Sat; M Liceu).

Walking Tour

Revelling in El Raval

El Raval is a neighbourhood whose contradictory impulses are legion. This journey through the local life of the barrio takes you from haunts beloved by the savvy young professionals moving into the area to gritty streetscapes and one-time slums frequented by Barcelona's immigrants and street-walkers. En route, we stop at places that, unlike the rest of the neighbourhood, haven't changed in decades.

Walk Facts

Start Bar Kasparo

End Bar Marsella

Length 2.1km; all day

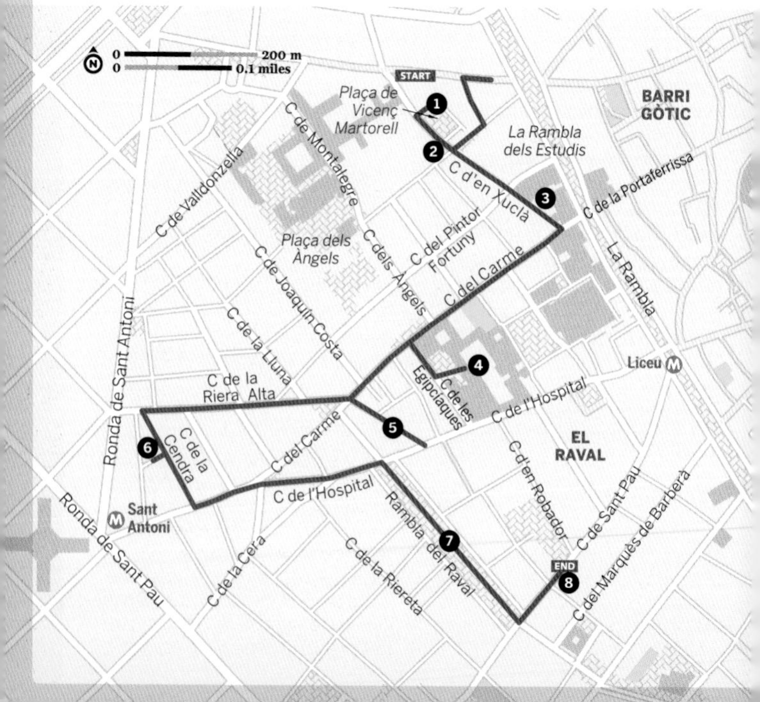

❶ A Neighbourhood Square

For a slice of local life, Plaça de Vicenç Martorell is difficult to beat. It's where the locals come to play with their kids or read the newspapers over a coffee or wine at **Bar Kasparo** (p67). Just a short hop from La Rambla, this is Barcelona as locals live it.

❷ Home-Style Cooking

Northern El Raval is rapidly gentrifying, but places like **Elisabets** (☎93 317 58 26; Carrer d'Elisabets 2-4; mains €8-10; ⏰7.30am-11.30pm Mon-Thu & Sat, to 1.30am Fri Sep-Jul; M Catalunya) hold firm. The walls are lined with old radio sets and the lunch menu varies daily. If you prefer à la carte, try the *ragú de jabalí* (wild boar stew) and finish with *mel i mató* (a Catalan dessert made from cheese and honey).

❸ Homemade Hot Chocolate

The fifth generation of its founding family runs **Granja M Viader** (p69), an atmospheric milk bar and cafe established in 1873. This place invented Cacaolat, the chocolate-and-skimmed-milk drink now popular all over Spain. Try a cup of homemade hot chocolate and whipped cream (ask for a *suís*).

❹ Garden of Earthly Delights

Drop into the courtyard and garden of the **Antic Hospital de la Santa Creu** (p66) and play on the giant chessboard, check out the book crossing service or have a glass of wine at the bar.

❺ Preloved Shopping

Looking for fashion bargains that are perfect for passing unnoticed in this 'hood? In little more than 100m along Carrer de la Riera Baixa, from Carrer del Carme to Carrer de l'Hospital, you'll find a wide variety of clothes shops, mostly selling secondhand.

❻ Live Music

Run by the Taller de Músics (Musicians' Workshop), the tiny **Jazz Sí Club** (p70) hosts a varied line-up, from jazz jams through to some good flamenco (Friday nights). Thursday night is Cuban night. Concerts start around 8.30pm or so, but arrive early to get a good spot.

❼ Scenic Stroll

For a wide cross-section of the neighbourhood's multicultural mix, take a stroll down the palm-lined **Rambla del Raval**. Flanked by restaurants and outdoor cafes, this promenade is Barcelona's newest *rambla* (laid out in 1995). Don't miss the enormous, whiskered *Gat (Cat)* sculpture by Colombian artist Fernando Botero, a favourite meeting spot in El Raval.

❽ Late-Night Drinks

End the day at **Bar Marsella** (p69), which opened in 1820 and has barely changed since; assorted chandeliers, tiles and mirrors decorate its one rambunctious room. As in Hemingway's time, absinthe is the drink of choice, which should give you a warm glow – though treat this potent libation with respect!

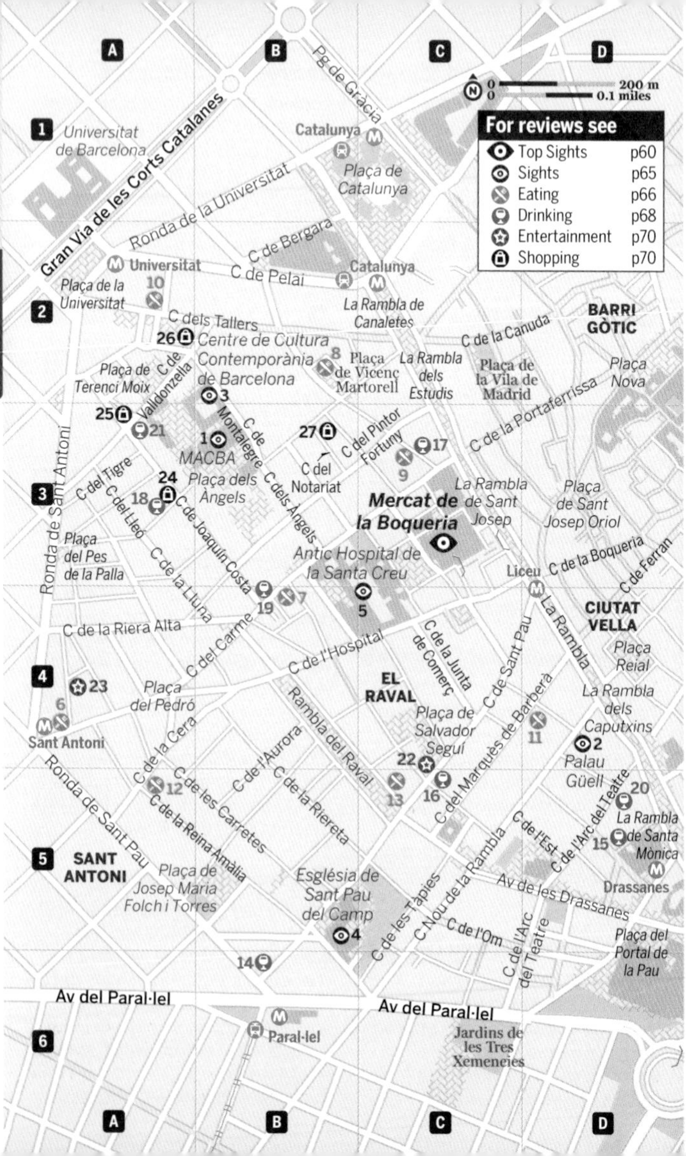
A
B
C
D
1
2
3
4
5
6
200 m
0.1 miles
For reviews see
Top Sights p60
Sights p65
Eating p66
Drinking p68
Entertainment p70
Shopping p70
Universitat de Barcelona
Gran Via de les Corts Catalanes
Pg de Gràcia
Catalunya
Plaça de Catalunya
Ronda de la Universitat
C de Bergara
Universitat
C de Pelai
Catalunya
Plaça de la Universitat
10
La Rambla de Canaletes
C dels Tallers
26
Centre de Cultura Contemporània de Barcelona
8
Plaça de Vicenç Martorell
La Rambla dels Estudis
C de la Canuda
BARRI GÒTIC
Plaça de la Vila de Madrid
Plaça Nova
Plaça de Terenci Moix
C de Valldonzella
3
C de la Portaferrissa
25
21
1
MACBA
C de Montalegre
27
C del Pintor Fortuny
17
9
C del Notariat
Ronda de Sant Antoni
C del Tigre
24
Plaça dels Àngels
C dels Àngels
La Rambla de Sant Josep
Plaça de Sant Josep Oriol
18
C del Lleó
C de Joaquín Costa
Mercat de la Boqueria
Plaça del Pes de la Palla
C de la Lluna
Antic Hospital de la Santa Creu
Liceu
C de la Boqueria
C de Ferran
19
7
5
La Rambla
CIUTAT VELLA
C de la Riera Alta
C del Carme
C de l'Hospital
C de la Junta de Comerç
C de Sant Pau
Plaça Reial
23
Plaça del Pedró
EL RAVAL
La Rambla dels Caputxins
6
Sant Antoni
C de la Cera
Rambla del Raval
Plaça de Salvador Seguí
C del Marquès de Barberà
11
2
Palau Güell
Ronda de Sant Pau
C de l'Aurora
22
12
C de les Carretes
C de la Riereta
13
16
20
C de la Reina Amàlia
C de l'Est
C de l'Arc del Teatre
La Rambla de Santa Mònica
15
SANT ANTONI
Plaça de Josep Maria Folch i Torres
Església de Sant Pau del Camp
C Nou de la Rambla
C de les Tàpies
Av de les Drassanes
Drassanes
4
C de l'Om
C de l'Arc del Teatre
Plaça del Portal de la Pau
14
Av del Paral·lel
Av del Paral·lel
Paral·lel
Jardins de les Tres Xemeneies

Sights

MACBA

ARTS CENTRE

1 MAP P64, B3

Designed by Richard Meier and opened in 1995, MACBA has become the city's foremost contemporary art centre, with captivating exhibitions for the serious art lover. The permanent collection is on the ground floor and dedicates itself to Spanish and Catalan art from the second half of the 20th century, with works by Antoni Tàpies, Joan Brossa and Miquel Barceló, among others, though international artists, such as Paul Klee, Bruce Nauman and John Cage, are also represented. (Museu d'Art Contemporani de Barcelona; 93 412 08 10; www.macba.cat; Plaça dels Àngels 1; adult/concession/child under 14yr €10/8/free; 11am-7.30pm Mon & Wed-Fri, 10am-9pm Sat, 10am-3pm Sun & holidays; M Universitat)

Palau Güell

PALACE

2 MAP P64, D4

Palau Güell is a magnificent example of the early days of Gaudí's fevered architectural imagination. The extraordinary neo-Gothic mansion, one of the few major buildings of that era raised in Ciutat Vella, gives an insight into its maker's prodigious genius. (93 472 57 71; www.palauguell.cat; Carrer Nou de la Rambla 3-5; adult/concession/child under 10yr incl audioguide €12/9/free, 1st Sun of month free; 10am-8pm Tue-Sun Apr-Oct, to 5.30pm Nov-Mar; M Drassanes)

Interior of MACBA

JOAN_BAUTISTA/SHUTTERSTOCK ©

Centre de Cultura Contemporània de Barcelona GALLERY

3 MAP P64, B2

A complex of auditoriums, exhibition spaces and conference halls opened here in 1994 in what had been an 18th-century hospice, the Casa de la Caritat. The courtyard, with a vast glass wall on one side, is spectacular. With 4500 sq metres of exhibition space in four separate areas, the centre hosts a constantly changing program of exhibitions, film cycles and other events. (CCCB; 93 306 41 00; www.cccb.org; Carrer de Montalegre 5; adult/concession/child under 12yr for 1 exhibition €6/4/free, 2 exhibitions €8/6/free, Sun 3-8pm free; 11am-8pm Tue-Sun; M Universitat)

Església de Sant Pau del Camp CHURCH

4 MAP P64, B5

The best example of Romanesque architecture in the city is the dainty little cloister of this church. Set in a somewhat dusty garden, the 12th-century church also boasts some Visigothic sculptural detail on the main entrance. (93 441 00 01; Carrer de Sant Pau 101; adult/concession/child under 14yr €3/2/free; 10am-1.30pm & 4-7.30pm Mon-Sat; M Paral·lel)

Antic Hospital de la Santa Creu HISTORIC BUILDING

5 MAP P64, C4

Behind La Boqueria stands the Antic Hospital de la Santa Creu, which was once the city's main hospital. Founded in 1401, it functioned until the 1930s, and was considered one of the best in Europe in its medieval heyday – it is famously the place where Antoni Gaudí died in 1926. Today it houses the **Biblioteca de Catalunya** and the **Institut d'Estudis Catalans** (Institute for Catalan Studies; 93 270 16 20; www.iec.cat; Carrer del Carme 47; 8am-8pm Mon-Fri Sep-Jul; M Liceu). The hospital's 15th-century former chapel, **La Capella** (93 256 20 44; www.bcn.cat/lacapella; Carrer de l'Hospital 56; admission free; noon-8pm Tue-Sat, 11am-2pm Sun & holidays; M Liceu), shows temporary exhibitions. (Former Hospital of the Holy Cross; www.barcelonaturisme.com; Carrer de l'Hospital 56; admission free; 9am-10pm; M Liceu)

Eating

Sésamo VEGETARIAN €

6 MAP P64, A4

Widely held to be the best veggie restaurant in the city (admittedly not as great an accolade as it might be elsewhere), Sésamo is a cosy, fun place. The menu is mainly tapas, and most people go for the seven-course tapas menu (€25, wine included), but there are a few more substantial dishes. Nice touches include the home-baked bread and cakes. (93 441 64 11; Carrer de Sant Antoni Abat 52; mains €9-13; 7pm-midnight Tue-Sun; ; M Sant Antoni)

Bar Muy Buenas

CATALAN €

7 MAP P64, B4

After a couple of years in the doldrums, the Modernista classic Muy Buenas, which has been a bar since 1924, is back on its feet and under new ownership. Its stunning and sinuous century-old woodwork has been meticulously restored, as have its etched-glass windows and marble bar. These days it's more restaurant than bar, though the cocktails are impressive. (93 807 28 57; Carrer del Carme 63; mains €9-13; 1-3.30pm & 8-11pm Sun-Thu, 1-4pm & 8-11.30pm Fri & Sat; M Liceu)

Bar Kasparo

CAFE €

8 MAP P64, B2

This friendly outdoor cafe, which overlooks a traffic-free square with a playground, is a favourite with the neighbourhood parents and serves juices, tapas and salads, as well as more substantial dishes from around the globe. (93 302 20 72; www.kasparo.es; Plaça de Vicenç Martorell 4; mains €7-11; 9am-11pm Tue-Sat, to midnight Jun-Sep; ; M Catalunya)

Gats

FUSION €€

9 MAP P64, C3

A relatively recent addition to the *barri*, Gats has been an instant hit, and its terrace is constantly full. A deliciously fresh spread of dishes ranges from baba ganoush to Thai green curry, but there's plenty here that's local – try the 'mountain paella' with sausage, or the smoked sardines with honey and truffle. The kitchen is open all day. (93 144 00 44; www.encompaniadelobos.com; Carrer d'en Xuclà 7; mains €9-19; noon-midnight; ; M Liceu)

Articket

Barcelona's best bargain for art lovers is the **Articket BCN** (www.articketbcn.org; €30), which gives you entry to six museums for a fraction of what you'd pay if you bought individual tickets. The museums are the **MACBA** (p65), **CCCB** (p66), **Fundació Antoni Tàpies** (p179), **Fundació Joan Miró** (p179), **MNAC** (p179) and **Museu Picasso** (p179).

Flax & Kale

VEGETARIAN €€

10 MAP P64, A2

A far cry from the veggie restaurants of old, Flax & Kale marks a new approach (for Barcelona, at least) that declares that going meat-free does not mean giving up on choice, creativity or style. There are gluten-free and vegan options, and dishes include tacos with guacamole, aubergine and sour cashew cream, or Penang red curry. (93 317 56 64; www.teresacarles.com; Carrer dels Tallers 74; mains €13-18; 9.30am-11.30pm Mon-Fri, from 10am Sat & Sun; ; M Universitat)

Bar Cañete

TAPAS €€

11 MAP P64, D4

Part of a trend in creating upmarket versions of traditional bars with food to match. A long, narrow dining room holds an open kitchen along which runs a wooden bar, where diners sit – from here, they can point at what they want or order from a long list of classic tapas and *platillos* (plates for sharing). (93 270 34 58; www.barcanete.com; Carrer de la Unió 17; tapas from €4.50; 1pm-midnight Mon-Sat; ; M Liceu)

Can Lluís

CATALAN €€

12 MAP P64, A5

Three generations have kept this spick-and-span old-time classic in business since 1929. Beneath the olive-green beams in the back dining room you can see the spot where an anarchist's bomb went off in 1946, killing the then owner. The restaurant is still going strong, however, with excellent seafood dishes and a good *menú del día* for €10.90. (93 441 11 87; www.restaurantcanlluis.cat; Carrer de la Cera 49; mains €14-16; 1.30-4pm & 8.30-11.30pm Mon-Sat; M Sant Antoni)

Suculent

CATALAN €€€

13 MAP P64, C5

Celebrity chef Carles Abellan adds to his stable with this old-style bistro, which showcases the best of Catalan cuisine. From the cod brandade to the oxtail stew with truffled sweet potato, only the best ingredients are used. There is no à la carte, just four different tasting menus to choose from. (93 443 65 79; www.suculent.com; Rambla del Raval 43; tasting menus €45-75; 1-4pm & 8-11.30pm Wed-Sun; ; M Liceu)

Drinking

La Confitería

BAR

14 MAP P64, B6

This is a trip into the 19th century. Until the 1980s it was a confectioner's shop, and although the original cabinets are now lined with booze, the look of the place barely changed with its conversion. A recent refurb of the back room is similarly sympathetic, and the vibe these days is lively cocktail bar. (93 140 54 35; Carrer de Sant Pau 128; 7pm-2.30am Mon-Thu, 6pm-3am Fri & Sat, 5pm-2.30am Sun; ; M Paral·lel)

Bar Pastís

BAR

15 MAP P64, D5

A French cabaret theme (with lots of Piaf on the stereo) pervades this tiny, cluttered classic, which has been going, on and off, since the end of WWII. You'll need to be in before 9pm to have any hope of sitting or getting near the bar. On some nights it features live acts, usually performing French *chanson*. (www.barpastis.es; Carrer de Santa Mònica 4; 8pm-2am Tue-Thu & Sun, to 3am Fri & Sat; ; M Drassanes)

Bar Marsella

BAR

16 MAP P64, C5

Bar Marsella has been in business since 1820, and has served the likes of Hemingway, who was known to slump here over an *absenta* (absinthe). The bar still specialises in absinthe, a drink to be treated with respect. (93 442 72 63; Carrer de Sant Pau 65; 10pm-2.30am Mon-Thu, to 3am Fri & Sat; M Liceu)

Granja M Viader

CAFE

17 MAP P64, C3

For more than a century, people have been coming here for hot chocolate with whipped cream (ask for a *suís*) ladled out in this classically Catalan milk bar. In 1931, the Viader clan invented Cacaolat, a bottled chocolate milk drink, with iconic label design. The interior here is delightfully old-fashioned and the atmosphere always lively. (93 318 34 86; www.granjaviader.cat; Carrer d'en Xuclà 6; 9am-1pm & 5-9pm Mon-Sat; M Liceu)

Casa Almirall

BAR

18 MAP P64, A3

In business since the 1860s, this unchanged corner bar is dark and intriguing, with Modernista decor and a mixed clientele. There are some great original pieces in here, such as the marble counter, and the cast-iron statue of the muse of the Universal Exposition, held in Barcelona in 1888. (93 318 95 92; www.casaalmirall.com; Carrer de Joaquín Costa 33; 5.30pm-2am Mon-Wed, noon-2.30am Thu-Sat, noon-12.30am Sun; ; M Universitat)

Bar Marsella

33|45

BAR

19 MAP P64, B4

A super-trendy bar on a street that's not short of them, this place has excellent mojitos, a fashionable crowd and a frequently changing exhibition of art on the walls. There are DJs most nights, along with plenty of sofas and armchairs for a post-dancing slump. (93 187 41 38; www.3345.struments.com; Carrer de Joaquín Costa 4; 1pm-2am Sun-Mon, to 3am Fri & Sat; ; M Universitat)

Moog

CLUB

20 MAP P64, D5

This fun and minuscule club is a standing favourite with the down-town crowd. In the main dance area DJs dish out house, techno and electro, while upstairs you can groove to a nice blend of indie and occasional classic-pop throw-backs. (93 319 17 89; www.masimas.com/moog; Carrer de l'Arc del Teatre 3; entry €5-10; midnight-5am Sun-Thu, to 6am Fri & Sat; M Drassanes)

Betty Ford's

BAR

21 MAP P64, A3

This enticing corner bar is one of several good stops along the student-jammed run of Carrer de Joaquín Costa. It puts together some nice cocktails and the place fills with an even mix of locals and foreigners, generally aged not much over 30. There's a decent line in burgers and soups, too. (93 304 13 68; Carrer de Joaquín Costa 56; 1pm-2.30am Tue-Sat, from 5pm Sun & Mon; ; M Universitat)

Entertainment

Filmoteca de Catalunya

CINEMA

22 MAP P64, C4

The Filmoteca de Catalunya – Catalonia's national cinema – sits in a modern 6000-sq-metre building in the midst of the most louche part of El Raval. The films shown are a superior mix of classics and more recent releases, with frequent themed cycles. A 10-session pass is an amazingly cheap €20. (93 567 10 70; www.filmoteca.cat; Plaça de Salvador Seguí 1-9; adult/concession €4/3; screenings 5-10pm, ticket office 10am-3pm & 4-9.30pm Tue-Sun; M Liceu)

Jazz Sí Club

LIVE MUSIC

23 MAP P64, A4

A cramped little bar run by the Taller de Músics (Musicians' Workshop) serves as the stage for a varied program of jazz jams through to some good flamenco (Friday and Saturday nights). Thursday night is Cuban night, Tuesday and Sunday are rock, and the rest are devoted to jazz and/or blues sessions. Concerts start around 9pm but the jam sessions can get going earlier. (93 329 00 20; www.tallerdemusics.com/en/jazzsi-club; Carrer de Requesens 2; entry incl drink €6-10; 8.30-11pm Tue-Sat, 6.30-10pm Sun; M Sant Antoni)

Shopping

Les Topettes

COSMETICS

24 MAP P64, A3

It's a sign of the times that such a chic little temple to soap and perfume can exist in El Raval. The items in Les Topettes' collection have been picked for their designs as much as for the products themselves, and you'll find gorgeously packaged scents, candles and unguents from Diptyque, Cowshed and L'Artisan Parfumeur, among others. (93 500 55 64; www.lestopettes.com; Carrer de Joaquín Costa 33; 11am-2pm & 4-9pm Tue-Sat, 4-9pm Mon; M Universitat)

Fantastik ARTS & CRAFTS

25 MAP P64, A3

Over 400 products, including a Mexican skull rattle, robot moon explorer from China and recycled plastic zebras from South Africa, are to be found in this colourful shop, which sources its items from Mexico, India, Bulgaria, Russia, Senegal and 20 other countries. It's a perfect place to buy all the things you don't need but can't live without. (93 301 30 68; www.fantastik.es; Carrer de Joaquín Costa 62; 11am-2pm & 4-8.30pm Mon-Fri, 11am-3pm & 4-9pm Sat; M Universitat)

Holala! Plaza FASHION & ACCESSORIES

26 MAP P64, A2

Backing on to Carrer de Valldonzella, where it boasts an exhibition space (Gallery) for temporary art displays, this Ibiza import is inspired by that island's long-established (and somewhat commercialised) hippie tradition. Vintage clothes are the name of the game, along with an eclectic program of exhibitions and activities. (www.holala-ibiza.com; Plaça de Castella 2; 11am-9pm Mon-Sat; M Universitat)

Reviving El Raval

The relocation of the **Filmoteca de Catalunya** (p70) to El Raval from the neighbourhood of Sarrià is part of the 'Raval Cultural', an ongoing project to set up the neighbourhood as one of Spain's most influential cultural centres. As part of the project, representatives from the MACBA, Gran Teatre del Liceu, Centre de Cultura Contemporània de Barcelona, Biblioteca de Catalunya, Arts Santa Mònica, Virreina Centre de la Imatge, Institut d'Estudis Catalans and Filmoteca de Catalunya work together to sustain a cultural network with El Raval as its nucleus. The project includes complementary exhibitions, cultural events, tours and collaboration in educational projects.

Teranyina ARTS & CRAFTS

27 MAP P64, B3

Artist Teresa Rosa Aguayo runs this textile workshop in the heart of the artsy bit of El Raval. You can join courses at the loom, admire some of the rugs and other works that Teresa has created, and, of course, buy them. (93 317 94 36; www.textilteranyina.com; Carrer del Notariat 10; 11am-2pm & 5-8pm Mon-Fri; M Catalunya)

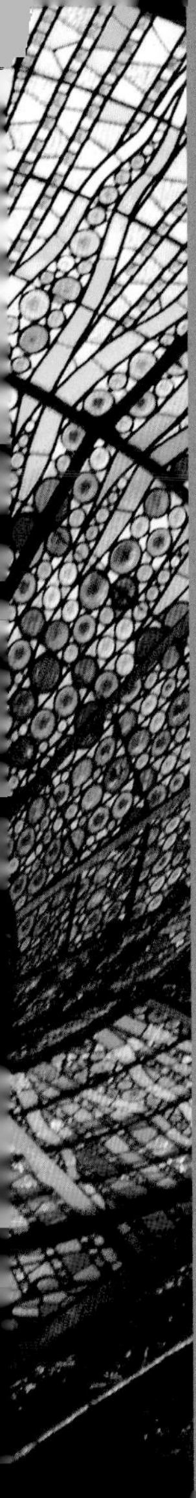

Explore

La Ribera & Parc de la Ciutadella

This medieval quarter has a little of everything, from high-end shopping to lively tapas bars. Key sights include the superb Museu Picasso, the awe-inspiring Gothic Basílica de Santa Maria del Mar and the artfully sculpted Modernista concert hall of Palau de la Música Catalana.

In a bid to avoid the crowds, get to the Museu Picasso (p74) early, then take a guided tour of the Palau de la Música Catalana (p84) to fully appreciate the genius and eccentricity of Modernisme. The Mercat de Santa Caterina (p84) is perfect for stocking up for a picnic lunch in the Parc de la Ciutadella (p86).

Explore the park after lunch, then settle into a pew to admire the grace and splendour of the Basílica de Santa Maria del Mar (p78). The church is just as beautiful on the outside, so make for our favourite vantage point, La Vinya del Senyor (p79), until evening falls.

The dining options in El Born are limitless, but we'd start with tapas at Euskal Etxea (p87), followed by Asturian dishes at El Chigre (p88). After dinner, enjoy a nightcap at glamorous Paradiso (p86).

Getting There

M Línia 4 coasts down the southwest flank of La Ribera, stopping at Urquinaona, Jaume I and Barceloneta. Línia 1 also stops nearby, at Urquinaona and Arc de Triomf (the nearest stop for the Parc de la Ciutadella).

Neighbourhood Map on p82

Palau de la Música Catalana (p84) ISABEL TALLEDA GUERRERO/GETTY IMAGES ©

Top Sight

Museu Picasso

Pablo Picasso spent many years in Barcelona and the museum is dedicated to the artist's formative years; the cubist paintings for which he is best known are largely absent, but this is nonetheless a world-class gallery that traces his development as an artist. The building – five contiguous medieval stone mansions that span five centuries and yet have seamlessly become one – is itself a perfectly conceived work of art.

MAP P82, D4

www.museupicasso.bcn.cat

Carrer de Montcada 15-23

adult/concession/child under 16yr all collections €14/7.50/free, permanent collection €11/7/free

9am-7pm Tue-Sun, to 9.30pm Thu

M Jaume I

History of the Museum

Allegedly it was Picasso himself who proposed the museum's creation to his friend and personal secretary Jaume Sabartés, a Barcelona native, in 1960. Three years later, the 'Sabartés Collection' was opened, since a museum bearing Picasso's name would have been met with censorship – Picasso's opposition to the Franco regime was well known. The Museu Picasso we see today opened in 1983. It originally held only Sabartés' personal collection of Picasso's art and a handful of works hanging at the Barcelona Museum of Art, but the collection gradually expanded with donations from Salvador Dalí and Sebastià Junyer i Vidal, among others, though most artworks were bequeathed by Picasso himself. His widow, Jacqueline Roque, also donated 41 ceramic pieces and the *Woman with Bonnet* painting after Picasso's death.

Sabartés' contribution and years of service are honoured with an entire room devoted to him, including Picasso's famous Blue Period portrait of him wearing a ruff.

The Collection

The collection concentrates on the artist's formative years in Barcelona and elsewhere in Spain, yet there is enough material from subsequent periods to give you a thorough impression of the man's versatility and genius. Above all, you come away feeling that Picasso was the true original, always one step ahead of himself (let alone anyone else) in his search for new forms of expression. The collection includes more than 3500 artworks, largely pre-1904, which is apt considering the artist spent his formative creative years in Barcelona.

It is important, however, not to expect a parade of his well-known works, or even works representative of his best-known periods. What makes this collection truly

★ Top Tips

- At €15, the Carnet del Museu Picasso annual pass is barely more expensive than a day pass, and allows multiple entries. There is a special desk for this, separate from the general ticket desk.
- Avoid queues by booking tickets online and choosing a time slot.
- Fares for temporary exhibitions vary, but you can see them for free from 6-9.30pm on Thursdays and on the first Sunday of the month.

✕ Take a Break

On Picasso's last visit to the city in 1934, El Xampanyet (p89) had already been open five years; it's still great for tapas.

impressive – and unique among the many Picasso museums around the world – is the way in which it displays his extraordinary talent at such a young age. Faced with the technical virtuosity of a painting such as *Ciència i caritat* (Science and Charity), for example, it is almost inconceivable that such a work could have been created by the hands of a 15-year-old. Some of his self-portraits and the portraits of his parents, which date from 1896, are also evidence of his precocious talent.

Early Barcelona Days

Rooms 1 and 2 hold sketches and oils from Picasso's early years in Málaga and A Coruña – around 1893–95, and lead on to his formative years in Barcelona. *Retrato de la tía Pepa* (Portrait of Aunt Pepa), done in Málaga in 1896, shows the maturity of his brush strokes and his ability to portray character – at the tender age of 15. As you walk into room 3, you'll see the enormous *Ciència i caritat* (Science and Charity), painted in the same year.

The Catalan Avant-Garde

After a period spent in Horta de Sant Joan, Picasso came to Barcelona and joined what was known as the 'Catalan avant-garde', which you'll see in room 4. In rooms 5–7 paintings from 1900–1901 hang, while room 8 is dedicated to the first significant new stage in his development, the Blue Period. *Woman with Bonnet* is an important work from this period, depicting a detainee from the Saint-Lazare women's prison and venereal disease hospital, which Picasso visited when in Paris – this also sets up the theme of Picasso's fascination with those inhabiting the down-and-out layers of society.

Museu Picasso

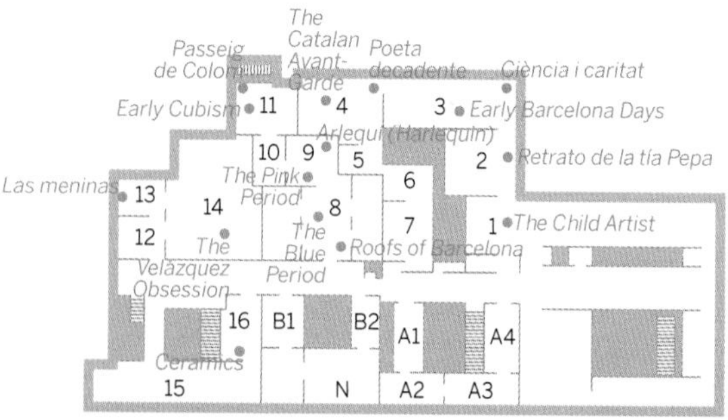

Early Cubism

Picasso did many drawings of beggars, the blind and the impoverished elderly throughout 1903 and 1904. This leads to the painting of Benedetta Bianco, from Picasso's Pink Period (in room 9), and thence on to the beginnings of cubism. Though the Museu Picasso is no showcase for his cubist period, it does hold a few examples; check out the *Glass and Tobacco Packet* still-life painting, a beautiful and simple work that marks the beginning of his fascination with still life.

Las Meninas Through the Prism of Picasso

From 1954 to 1962 Picasso was obsessed with the idea of researching and 'rediscovering' the greats, in particular Velázquez. In 1957 he created a series of renditions of the Velázquez masterpiece *Las meninas* (The Ladies-in-Waiting), now displayed in rooms 12–14. It is as though Picasso has looked at the original Velázquez painting through a prism reflecting all the styles he had worked through until then, creating his own masterpiece in the process. This is a wonderful opportunity to see *Las meninas* in its entirety in this beautiful space.

Getting Around the Collection

The permanent collection is housed in Palau Aguilar, Palau del Baró de Castellet and Palau Meca. Casa Mauri and the adjacent 14th-century Palau Finestres accommodate temporary exhibitions.

Ceramics

What is also special about the Museu Picasso is its showcasing of his work in lesser-known media. The last rooms contain engravings and some 40 ceramic pieces completed throughout the latter years of his unceasingly creative life. You'll see plates and bowls decorated with simple, single-line drawings of fish, owls and other animal shapes, typical of Picasso's daubing on clay.

Top Sight

Basílica de Santa Maria del Mar

At one end of Passeig del Born stands the apse of Barcelona's finest Catalan Gothic church, Santa Maria del Mar (Our Lady of the Sea). Its construction started in 1329, with Berenguer de Montagut and Ramon Despuig as the architects. Famously the parishioners themselves gave up their time to help construct the church, particularly the stevedores from the nearby port.

MAP P82, D5

93 310 23 90

www.santamariadelmar barcelona.org

Plaça de Santa Maria del Mar

€8 1-5pm, incl guided tour

9am-8.30pm Mon-Sat, 10am-8pm Sun

M Jaume I

Main Sanctuary

The pleasing unity of form and symmetry of the church's central nave and two flanking aisles owed much to the rapidity with which the church was built – a mere 54 years, which must be a record for a major European house of worship. The slender, octagonal pillars create an enormous sense of lateral space bathed in the light of stained glass.

Ceiling and Side Chapels

Even before anarchists gutted the church in 1909 and again in 1936, Santa Maria always lacked superfluous decoration. Gone are the gilded chapels that weigh heavily over so many Spanish churches, while the splashes of colour high above the nave are subtle – unusually and beautifully so. It all serves to highlight the church's fine proportions, purity of line and sense of space.

The Porters

Look closely at the stones throughout the main sanctuary. One day a week during construction, the city's *bastaixos* (porters) carried these stones on their backs from the royal quarry in Montjuïc to the construction site. The memory of them lives on in reliefs in the main doors and stone carvings in the church, a reminder that this was conceived as a people's church.

★ Top Tips

- Take a guided tour (offered 1pm to 5pm) to visit the roof terrace and crypt (€8).
- If your purpose is spiritual, try to be here for the daily mass at 7.30pm.
- Ask in the gift shop in case evening baroque music recitals are scheduled.

Take a Break

Admire the western facade of the church while enjoying tapas and drinks at one of the outdoor tables of **La Vinya del Senyor** (93 310 33 79; Plaça de Santa Maria del Mar 5; noon-1am Mon-Thu, to 2am Fri & Sat, to midnight Sun; ; M Jaume I).

Treat yourself to coffee and a cake at nearby **Bubó** (93 268 72 24; www.bubo.es; Carrer de les Caputxes 6 & 10; tapas from €4; h10am-9pm Mon-Thu, to 11pm Fri & Sat, 10am-10pm Sun; M Barceloneta).

Walking Tour

Tapas & Bar Hopping in El Born

If there's one place that distils Barcelona's enduring cool to its essence and provides a snapshot of all that's irresistible about this city, it has to be El Born, the tangle of streets surrounding the Basílica de Santa Maria del Mar. Its secret is simple: this is where locals go for an authentic Barcelona night out.

Walk Facts

Start Passeig del Born

End Cactus Bar

Length 1.1km; 3–6 hours

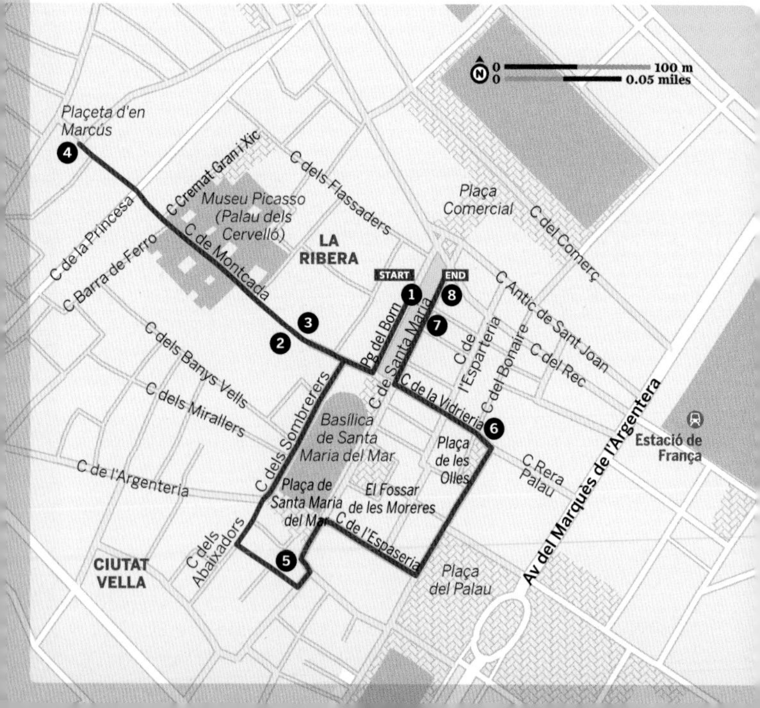

❶ Passeig del Born

Most nights, and indeed most things, in El Born begin along **Passeig del Born**, one of the prettiest little boulevards in Europe. It's a place to sit as much as to promenade. It's a graceful setting beneath the trees from which El Born's essential appeal is obvious – thronging people, brilliant bars and architecture that springs from a medieval film set.

❷ Catalan Tapas

Push through the crowd to order a *cava* (sparkling wine) and an assortment of tapas at **El Xampanyet** (p89), one of the city's best-known *cava* bars, in business since 1929. Star dishes include tangy *boquerones en vinagre* (white anchovies in vinegar) and there's high-quality seafood served from a can in the Catalan way.

❸ Basque Delicacies

Having taken your first lesson in Barcelona-style tapas it's time to compare it with the *pintxos* (Basque tapas of food morsels perched atop pieces of bread) lined up along the bar at **Euskal Etxea** (p87), a real slice of San Sebastián.

❹ Spain with a Twist

This detour to the northern limits of El Born is worth the walk. At first glance, the tapas at informal **Bar del Pla** (p87) are traditionally Spanish, but the riffs on a theme display an assured touch. Try the squid ink croquettes or oxtail parcels with foie.

❺ Tapas with a View

Back in the heart of El Born is pastry chef Carles Mampel's **Bubó** (p79). If you're not already sated, try the salted cod croquettes at one of the outdoor tables inching onto the lovely square.

❻ An Enduring Star

Boisterous **Cal Pep** (☎93 310 79 61; www.calpep.com; Plaça de les Olles 8; mains €13-20; ⏲7.30-11.30pm Mon, 1-3.45pm & 7.30-11.30pm Tue-Sat, closed last 3 weeks Aug; Ⓜ Barceloneta) is one of Barcelona's lasting stars. It can be difficult to snaffle a bar stool from which to order gourmet bar snacks such as *cloïsses amb pernil* (clams with ham); so if it's full, order a drink and wait. It's always worth it.

❼ El Born's Favourite Bar

El Born Bar (☎93 319 53 33; www.elbornbar.com; Passeig del Born 26; ⏲10am-2am Mon-Thu, to 3am Fri & Sat, noon-2.30am Sun; Ⓜ Jaume I) effortlessly attracts everyone from cool thirty-somethings from all over town to locals who pass judgement on Passeig del Born's passing parade. Its staying power depends on a good selection of beers, spirits, and *empanadas* and other snacks.

❽ The Last Mojito

So many Barcelona nights end with a mojito, and El Born's biggest and best are to be found at **Cactus Bar** (☎93 247 92 90; Passeig del Born 30; ⏲3pm-3am Ⓜ Jaume I). The outdoor tables next to Passeig del Born are the perfect place to wind down.

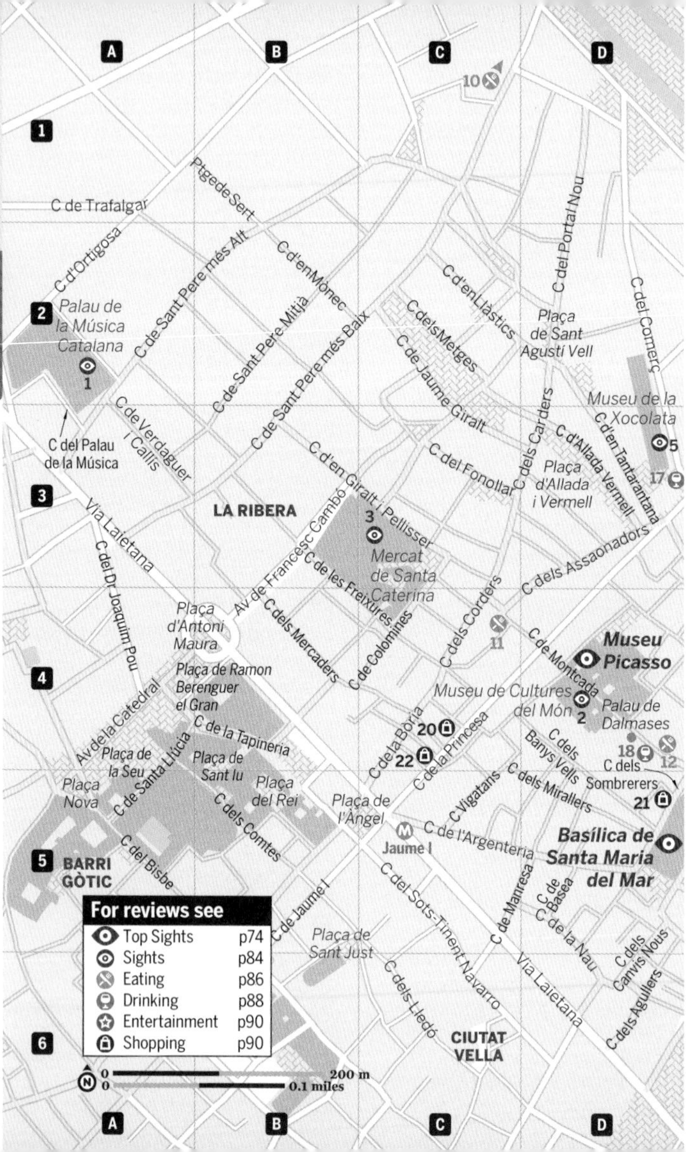
A
B
C
D
1
2
3
4
5
6
10
C de Trafalgar
Ptge de Sert
C d'Ortigosa
C de Sant Pere més Alt
C d'en Mònec
C del Portal Nou
C d'en Llàstics
C dels Metges
C de Jaume Giralt
C de Sant Pere Mitjà
C de Sant Pere més Baix
Palau de la Música Catalana
1
Plaça de Sant Agustí Vell
C del Comerç
Museu de la Xocolata
5
C d'en Tantarantana
C dels Carders
C d'Allada Vermell
Plaça d'Allada i Vermell
17
C del Fonollar
C de Verdaguer i Callís
C del Palau de la Música
C d'en Giralt i Pellisser
LA RIBERA
3
Mercat de Santa Caterina
Via Laietana
C del Dr Joaquim Pou
Av de Francesc Cambó
C de les Freixures
C dels Assaonadors
C dels Corders
11
Plaça d'Antoni Maura
C dels Mercaders
C de Colomines
C de Montcada
Museu Picasso
Plaça de Ramon Berenguer el Gran
Museu de Cultures del Món
2
Palau de Dalmases
Av de la Catedral
C de la Tapineria
C de la Bòria
20
22
C de la Princesa
C dels Banys Vells
18
12
C dels Sombrerers
Plaça de la Seu
C de Santa Llúcia
Plaça de Sant Iu
Plaça del Rei
Plaça de l'Àngel
C Vigatans
C dels Mirallers
21
Plaça Nova
C de Santa Llúcia
C dels Comtes
Jaume I
C de l'Argenteria
Basílica de Santa Maria del Mar
BARRI GÒTIC
C del Bisbe
C de Jaume I
C del Sots-Tinent Navarro
C de Manresa
C de Basea
C de la Nau
For reviews see
Top Sights p74
Sights p84
Eating p86
Drinking p88
Entertainment p90
Shopping p90
Plaça de Sant Just
C dels Lledó
Via Laietana
C dels Canvis Nous
C dels Agullers
CIUTAT VELLA
0 200 m
0 0.1 miles
N

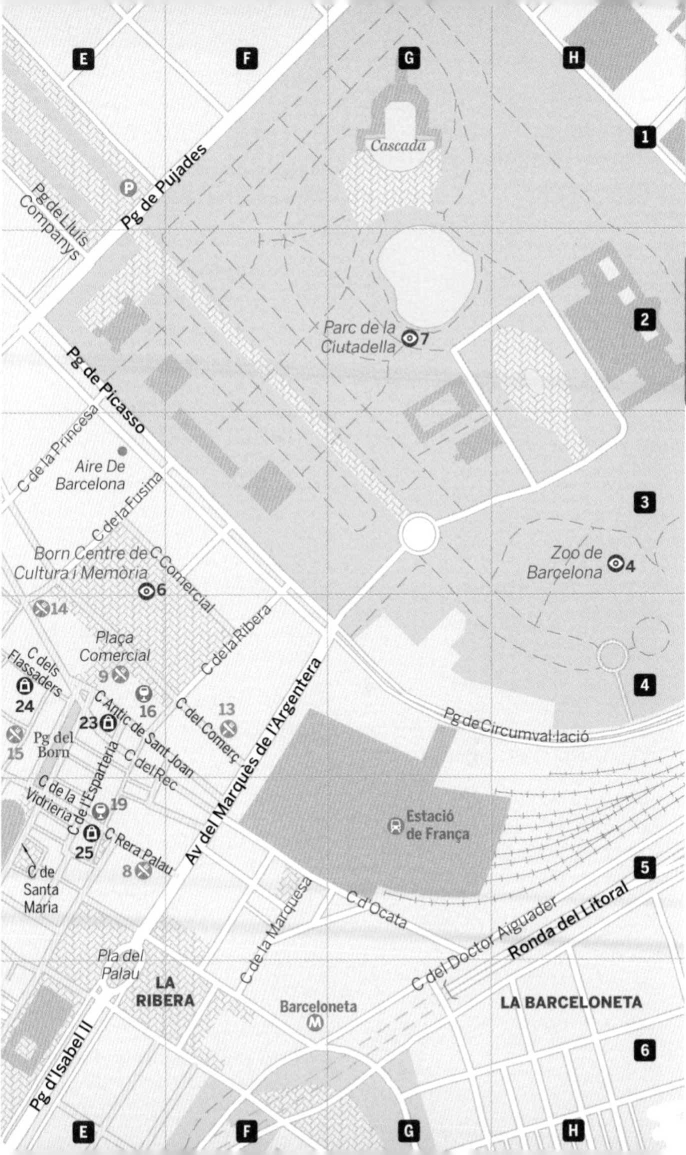
E
F
G
H
1
2
3
4
5
6
Cascada
Pg de Pujades
Pg de Lluís Companys
Parc de la Ciutadella
7
Pg de Picasso
C de la Princesa
Aire De Barcelona
C de la Fusina
Born Centre de Cultura i Memòria
6
C Comercial
14
Zoo de Barcelona
4
Plaça Comercial
C de la Ribera
C dels Flassaders
9
24
16
13
23
C Antic de Sant Joan
C del Comerç
Av del Marquès de l'Argentera
Pg de Circumval·lació
Pg del Born
15
C de l'Espartería
C del Rec
C de la Vidrieria
19
25
C Rera Palau
8
Estació de França
C de Santa Maria
C de la Marquesa
C d'Ocata
C del Doctor Aiguader
Ronda del Litoral
Pla del Palau
LA RIBERA
Barceloneta
LA BARCELONETA
Pg d'Isabel II

Sights

Palau de la Música Catalana

ARCHITECTURE

1 MAP P82, A2

This concert hall is a high point of Barcelona's Modernista architecture, a symphony in tile, brick, sculpted stone and stained glass. Built by Domènech i Montaner between 1905 and 1908 for the Orfeo Català musical society, it was conceived as a temple for the Catalan Renaixença (Renaissance). (93 295 72 00; www.palaumusica.cat; Carrer de Palau de la Música 4-6; adult/concession/child under 10yr €18/15/free; guided tours 10am-3.30pm, to 6pm Easter, Jul & Aug; M Urquinaona)

Museu de Cultures del Món

MUSEUM

2 MAP P82, D4

The Palau Nadal and the Palau Marquès de Llió, which once housed the Museu Barbier-Mueller and the Museu Tèxtil respectively, reopened in 2015 to the public as the site of the new Museum of World Cultures. Exhibits from private and public collections, including many from the Museu Etnològic on Montjuïc, take the visitor on a trip through the ancient cultures of Africa, Asia, the Americas and Oceania. There's a combined ticket with the Museu Egipci (p180) and Museu Etnològic (p168) for €12. (93 256 23 00; http://museuculturesmon.bcn.cat; Carrer de Montcada 12; adult/concession/under 16yr €5/3.50/free, temporary exhibition €2.20/1.50/free, 3-8pm Sun & 1st Sun of month free; 10am-7pm Tue-Sat, to 8pm Sun; M Jaume I)

Mercat de Santa Caterina

MARKET

3 MAP P82, C3

Come shopping for your tomatoes at this extraordinary-looking produce market, designed by Enric Miralles and Benedetta Tagliabue to replace its 19th-century predecessor. Finished in 2005, it is distinguished by its kaleidoscopic and undulating roof, held up above the bustling produce stands, restaurants, cafes and bars by twisting slender branches of what look like grey steel trees. (93 319 57 40; www.mercatsantacaterina.com; Avinguda de Francesc Cambó 16; 7.30am-3.30pm Mon, Wed & Sat, to 8.30pm Tue, Thu & Fri, closed afternoons Jul & Aug; M Jaume I)

Zoo de Barcelona

ZOO

4 MAP P82, H3

The zoo is a great day out for kids, with 7500 critters that range from geckos to gorillas, lions and elephants – there are more than 400 species, plus picnic areas dotted all around and a wonderful adventure playground. There are pony rides, a petting zoo and a minitrain meandering through the grounds. Thanks to recent advances in legislation prohibiting the use of animals for performances (including circuses and bullfighting) the zoo called time on its dolphin shows in late 2015. (902 457545; www.

zoobarcelona.cat; Parc de la Ciutadella; adult/concession/child under 3yr €20/12/free; 10am-5.30pm Nov-Mar, 10am-7pm Apr, May, Sep & Oct, 10am-8pm Jun-Aug; ; M Barceloneta)

Museu de la Xocolata MUSEUM

5 MAP P82, D3

Chocoholics have a hard time containing themselves in this museum dedicated to the fundamental foodstuff – particularly when faced with tempting displays of cocoa-based treats in the cafe at the exit. The displays trace the origins of chocolate, its arrival in Europe, and the many myths and images associated with it. Among the informative stuff and machinery used in the production of chocolate are large chocolate models of emblematic buildings such as La Sagrada Família, along with various characters, local and international. (93 268 78 78; www.museuxocolata.cat; Carrer del Comerç 36; adult/concession/child under 7yr €6/5/free; 10am-7pm Mon-Sat, 10am-3pm Sun; ; M Arc de Triomf)

Born Centre de Cultura i Memòria HISTORIC BUILDING

6 MAP P82, E3

Launched in 2013, as part of the events held for the tercentenary of the Catalan defeat in the War of the Spanish Succession, this cultural space is housed in the **former Mercat del Born**, a handsome 19th-century structure of slatted iron and brick. Excavation in 2001 unearthed remains of whole streets flattened to make way for the

Parc de la Ciutadella (p86)

SOPOTNICKI/SHUTTERSTOCK ©

Catalan Gothic

Catalan Gothic did not follow the same course as the style typical of northern Europe. Decoration here tends to be more sparing and the most obvious defining characteristic is the triumph of breadth over height. While northern European cathedrals reach for the sky, Catalan Gothic has a tendency to push to the sides, stretching its vaulting design to the limit.

The **Saló del Tinell** (p180), with a parade of 15m arches (among the largest ever built without reinforcement) holding up the roof, is a perfect example of Catalan Gothic. Another is the present home of the **Museu Marítim** (p98), the Drassanes, Barcelona's medieval shipyards. In their churches, too, the Catalans opted for a more robust shape and lateral space – step into the Basílica de Santa Maria del Mar or the **Basílica de Santa Maria del Pi** (p47) and you'll soon get the idea.

Another notable departure from what you might have come to expect of Gothic north of the Pyrenees is the lack of spires and pinnacles. Bell towers tend to terminate in a flat or nearly flat roof. Occasional exceptions prove the rule – the main facade of Barcelona's **La Catedral** (p44), with its three gnarled and knobbly spires, does vaguely resemble the outline that confronts you in cathedrals in Chartres or Cologne. But then it was a 19th-century addition, admittedly to a medieval design.

much-hated *ciutadella* (citadel) – these are now on show on the exposed subterranean level. (☎93 256 68 51; http://elbornculturaimemoria.barcelona.cat; Plaça Comercial 12; centre free, exhibition spaces adult/concession/child under 16yr €4.40/3/free; ⏰10am-8pm Tue-Sun Mar-Oct, 10am-7pm Tue-Sat, to 8pm Sun Nov-Feb; M Jaume I)

Parc de la Ciutadella PARK

7 MAP P82, G2

Come for a stroll, a picnic, a boat ride on the lake or to inspect Catalonia's parliament, but don't miss a visit to this, the most central green lung in the city. Parc de la Ciutadella is perfect for winding down. (Passeig de Picasso; ⏰8am-9pm May-Sep, to 7pm Oct-Apr; 👪; M Arc de Triomf)

Eating

Paradiso/Pastrami Bar SMOKERY, COCKTAIL BAR €

8 MAP P82, E5

A kind of Narnia-in-reverse, Paradiso is fronted with a snowy-white space, not much bigger than a wardrobe, with pastrami sandwiches, pulled pork and other home-cured delights. But this is only the portal – pull open the huge wooden fridge door, and step through into a glam, sexy speakeasy of a cocktail bar guaranteed to raise the most world-weary of eyebrows. (639 310671; www.rooftopsmokehouse.com; Carrer de Rera Palau 4; mains €7-9; 7pm-2am Mon-Thu, to 3am Fri & Sat; ; M Barceloneta)

Casa Delfín CATALAN €€

9 MAP P82, E4

One of Barcelona's culinary delights, Casa Delfín is everything you dream of when you think of Catalan (and Mediterranean) cooking. Start with the tangy and sweet *calçots* (spring onions; February and March only) or salt-strewn *Padrón* peppers, moving on to grilled sardines speckled with parsley, then tackle the meaty monkfish roasted in white wine and garlic. (93 319 50 88; www.facebook.com/Casa-Delfin-326525620764565/; Passeig del Born 36; mains €10-17; 8am-midnight Sun-Thu, to 1am Fri & Sat; ; M Jaume I)

Nakashita JAPANESE €€

10 MAP P82, C1

Brazil's particular immigration story means it has a tradition of superb Japanese food, and the Brazilian chef at Nakashita is no slouch, turning out excellent sashimi, maki rolls, softshell crab and *kakiage* (a mix of tempura). One of the best Japanese restaurants in the city, with just a handful of tables – book if you can. (93 295 53 78; www.nakashitabcn.com; Carrer del Rec Comtal 15; mains €12-22; 1.30-4pm & 8.30pm-midnight Mon-Sun; ; M Arc de Triomf)

Bar del Pla TAPAS €€

11 MAP P82, C4

A bright and occasionally rowdy place, with glorious Catalan tiling, a vaulted ceiling and bottles of wine lining the walls. At first glance, the tapas at informal Bar del Pla are traditionally Spanish, but the riffs on a theme display an assured touch. Try the ham croquettes, Wagyu burger, T-bone steak or marinated salmon, yoghurt and mustard. (93 268 30 03; www.bardelpla.cat; Carrer de Montcada 2; mains €12-16; noon-11pm Mon-Thu, to midnight Fri & Sat; ; M Jaume I)

Euskal Etxea TAPAS €

12 MAP P82, D4

Barcelona has plenty of Basque and pseudo-Basque tapas bars, but this is the real deal. It captures the feel of San Sebastián better than many of its newer competitors. Choose your *pintxos* (Basque tapas piled on slices of bread), sip *txakoli* (Basque white wine), and keep the toothpicks so the staff can count them up and work out your bill. (93 310 21 85; www.euskaletxeataberna.com; Placeta de Montcada 1; tapas €2.10; 10am-12.30am Sun-Thu, to 1am Fri & Sat; ; M Jaume I)

Koku Kitchen Buns ASIAN €

13 MAP P82, F4

Steamed buns stuffed with beef or pork with coriander, peanuts,

Squaring up to the Past

Antonio López y López was an entrepreneur and philanthropist, whose generosity funded the construction of most of the buildings at the port-end of the Via Laietana, where a square now bears his name. In recent years, it's emerged that some of his money was made from the slave trade, and there is a move to rename the square after Nelson Mandela, among other proposals.

The council is dragging its heels, however, so in the meantime, activists have covered the street sign with a plaque reading 'Plaça de Idrissa Diallo', named for a young Guinean immigrant who died in a local detention centre in 2012.

pickled fennel and a sake sauce are the big draw here, but the starters, sides and even the excellent home-made lemonade are also worthy of note, as is the list of inventive cocktails. A great-value lunch *menú del día* is €13. (93 269 65 36; www.kokukitchen.es; Carrer del Comerç 29; mains €9-11; 1-4pm & 7.30-11.30pm; ; M Barceloneta)

Bormuth

TAPAS €

14 MAP P82, E4

Bormuth has tapped into the vogue for old-school tapas with modern-day service and decor, and serves all the old favourites – *patatas bravas* (potatoes in a spicy tomato sauce), *ensaladilla* (Russian salad) and tortilla – along with some less predictable and superbly prepared numbers (try the chargrilled red pepper with black pudding). (93 310 21 86; Carrer del Rec 31; tapas €4-10; noon-1.30am Sun-Thu, to 2.30am Fri & Sat; ; M Jaume I)

El Chigre

TAPAS €€

15 MAP P82, E4

Styling itself as part Asturian cider house and part Catalan *vermuteria* (bar specialising in vermouth, served on ice with a slice of orange and a green olive), El Chigre brings sophisticated versions of classic dishes from both regions to its menu. Try the superb tomato and tuna salad with tomato *gelée*, or the puffed corn *tortos* with lamb stew. (93 782 63 30; http://elchigre1769.com; Carrer dels Sombrerers 7; mains €10-17; noon-11.45pm, from 1pm Mon-Fri Nov-Mar; M Jaume I)

Drinking

Guzzo

COCKTAIL BAR

16 MAP P82, E4

This swish but relaxed cocktail bar is run by much-loved Barcelona DJ Fred Guzzo, who is often to be found at the decks, spinning his delicious selection of funk, soul and rare groove. You'll also find frequent live-music acts of consistently decent quality, and a funky atmosphere at almost any time of day. (93 667 00 36; www.guzzoclub.es; Plaça Comercial 10; 6pm-2.30am Mon-Thu, to 3am Fri & Sat, noon-3am Sun; ; Jaume I)

Bar del Convent CAFE

17 MAP P82, D3

Alongside the Gothic arches of what remains of the Sant Agusti convent's cloister is this pleasant cafe-bar – particularly good for people with children. Kids often play football in the cloister grounds, and there are children's books and toys in the cafe itself. You can also enter at Carrer del Comerç 36 through James Turrell's light sculpture. (93 256 50 17; www.bardelconvent.com; Plaça de l'Acadèmia; 10am-9pm Tue-Sat; ; Arc de Triomf)

El Xampanyet WINE BAR

18 MAP P82, D4

Nothing has changed for decades in this, one of the city's best-known *cava* (wine) bars. Plant yourself at the bar or seek out a table against the decoratively tiled walls for a glass or three of the cheap house *cava* and an assortment of tapas, such as the tangy *boquerones en vinagre* (fresh anchovies in vinegar). (93 319 70 03; Carrer de Montcada 22; noon-3.30pm & 7-11.15pm Tue-Sat, noon-3.30pm Sun; ; Jaume I)

Mudanzas BAR

19 MAP P82, E5

This was one of the first bars to get things into gear in El Born and it still attracts a faithful crowd. With its chequered floor and marble-topped

Mercat de Santa Caterina (p84)

tables, it's an attractive, lively place for a beer and perhaps a sandwich or a tapa. It also has a nice line in rum and malt whisky. (93 319 11 37; Carrer de la Vidrieria 15; 8am-2.30am Mon-Fri, 10am-2.30am Sat & Sun; ; M Jaume I)

Entertainment

Palau de la Música Catalana CLASSICAL MUSIC

A feast for the eyes, this Modernista confection is also the city's most traditional venue for classical and choral music (see 1 Map p82, A2), although it has a wide-ranging program, including flamenco, pop and – particularly – jazz. Just being here for a performance is an experience. In the foyer, its tiled pillars all a-glitter, you can sip a pre-concert tipple. (93 295 72 00; www.palaumusica.cat; Carrer de Palau de la Música 4-6; tickets from €18; box office 9.30am-9pm Mon-Sat, 10am-3pm Sun; M Urquinaona)

A Medieval Concert Hall

You can sip wine or cocktails (both rather expensive) inside the baroque courtyard and theatrical interior of the originally medieval **Palau de Dalmases** (Map p82, D4; 93 310 06 73; www.palaudalmases.com; Carrer de Montcada 20; 6pm-2am Tue-Sat, 6-10pm Sun; M Jaume I). There are flamenco shows at 6pm, 7.30pm and 9.30pm (€25 including one drink). On Wednesdays there is a free jazz concert at 11pm, and on Thursdays opera (€20).

Shopping

El Rei de la Màgia MAGIC

20 MAP P82, C4

For more than 100 years, the owners have been keeping locals both astounded and amused. Should you decide to stay in Barcelona and make a living as a magician, this is the place to buy levitation brooms, glasses of disappearing milk and decks of magic cards. (93 319 39 20; www.elreydelamagia.com; Carrer de la Princesa 11; 10.30am-2pm & 4-7.30pm Mon-Sat; M Jaume I)

Casa Gispert FOOD

21 MAP P82, D5

The wonderful, atmospheric and wood-fronted Casa Gispert has been toasting nuts and selling all manner of dried fruit since 1851. Pots and jars piled high on the shelves contain an unending variety of crunchy titbits: some roasted, some honeyed, all of them moreish. Your order is shouted over to the till, along with the price, in a display of old-world accounting. (93 319 75 35; www.casagispert.com; Carrer dels Sombrerers 23; 10am-8.30pm Mon-Sat; M Jaume I)

Arlequí Màscares ARTS & CRAFTS

22 MAP P82, C4

A wonderful little oasis of originality, this shop specialises in masks for costume and decoration. Some of the pieces are superb, while stock also includes a beautiful range of decorative boxes in Catalan themes, and some old-style marionettes. (☎93 268 27 52; www.arlequimask.com; Carrer de la Princesa 7; ⏰11.30am-8pm Mon, 10.30am-8pm Tue-Fri, 11am-8pm Sat, 11.30am-7pm Sun; M Jaume I)

Coquette FASHION & ACCESSORIES

23 MAP P82, E4

With its spare, cut-back and designer look, this friendly fashion store is attractive in its own right. Women can browse through casual, feminine wear by such designers as Humanoid, Vanessa Bruno, UKE and Hoss Intropia and others, with a further collection nearby at **Carrer de Bonaire 5** (☎93 310 35 35). (☎93 319 29 76; www.coquettebcn.com; Carrer del Rec 65; ⏰11am-3pm & 5-9pm Mon-Fri, 11.30am-9pm Sat; M Barceloneta)

Loisaida CLOTHING, ANTIQUES

24 MAP P82, E4

A sight in its own right, housed in the former coach house and stables for the Royal Mint, Loisaida (from the Spanglish for 'Lower East Side') is a deceptively large emporium of colourful, retro and somewhat preppy clothing for men and women, costume jewellery, music from the 1940s and '50s and some covetable antiques. One space is devoted entirely to denim. (☎93 295 54 92; www.loisaidabcn.com; Carrer dels Flassaders 42; ⏰11am-9pm Mon-Sat, 11am-2pm & 4-8pm Sun; M Jaume I)

A Spa Afternoon

With low lighting and relaxing perfumes wafting around you, the **Aire De Barcelona** (Map p82, E3; ☎93 295 57 43; www.airedebarcelona.com; Passeig de Picasso 22; thermal baths & aromatherapy Mon-Thu €36, Fri-Sun €39; ⏰9am-11pm Sun-Thu, to midnight Fri & Sat; M Arc de Triomf) spa could be the perfect way to end a day. Hot, warm and cold baths, steam baths and options for various massages, including on a slab of hot marble, make for a delicious hour or so. Book ahead and bring a swimming costume.

Custo Barcelona FASHION & ACCESSORIES

25 MAP P82, E5

The psychedelic decor and casual atmosphere lend this avant-garde Barcelona fashion store a youthful edge. Custo presents daring new women's and men's collections each year on the New York catwalks. The dazzling colours and cut of everything from dinner jackets to hot pants are for the uninhibited. It has three other stores around town. (☎93 268 78 93; www.custo.com; Plaça de les Olles 7; ⏰noon-8.30pm Mon-Sat; M Barceloneta)

Explore

Barceloneta & the Beaches

Since the late 20th century, Barcelona's formerly industrial waterfront has experienced a dramatic transformation, with sparkling beaches and seaside restaurants, sculpture, a long boardwalk and yacht-filled marinas. The gateway to the Mediterranean is the gridlike neighbourhood of Barceloneta, an old-fashioned fishing quarter full of traditional seafood restaurants, flanked by a palm-lined promenade leading to the beaches.

Begin with a journey through Catalan history at the Museu d'Història de Catalunya (p98), take a return trip aboard the Teleférico del Puerto (p179) for fine waterfront views, then head for L'Aquàrium (p98), one of Spain's best aquariums.

Most afternoons in Barceloneta revolve around food and beaches. For the former, we suggest a feast of small plates of seafood at Kaiku (p102) or La Cova Fumada (p101). The perfect response to such gastronomic excess is to lie down, and this is best done at any beach that takes your fancy from Barceloneta to Port Olímpic and beyond.

There are loads of great settings for a drink in the area. Festive Can Paixano (p103) has ever-flowing glasses of cava (sparkling wine), while Poblenou has the wonderful Balius (p104). For Mediterranean views, opt for one of the summertime chiringuitos, where you can sip cocktails while digging your heels in the sand.

Getting There & Around

M Go to Drassanes (Línia 3) to reach Port Vell; Barceloneta (Línia 4) has its own stop for the neighbourhood. Línia 4 continues out to Ciutadella Vila Olímpica (the best stop for Port Olímpic), the city's northern beaches and El Maresme Fòrum.

Neighbourhood Map on p96

A cable car tower in Barceloneta JENS SIEWERT/SHUTTERSTOCK ©

Walking Tour

Barceloneta's Sea & Seafood

Barcelona's Mediterranean roots are nowhere more pronounced than in Barceloneta, a seaside peninsula with a salty air and an enduring relationship with the sea. As often as not, this is one area where locals outnumber tourists, at least on weekends when the city's restaurants and beaches throng with a predominantly local crowd.

Walk Facts

Start Can Paixano

End Port Olímpic

Length 3.8km; as long as you like!

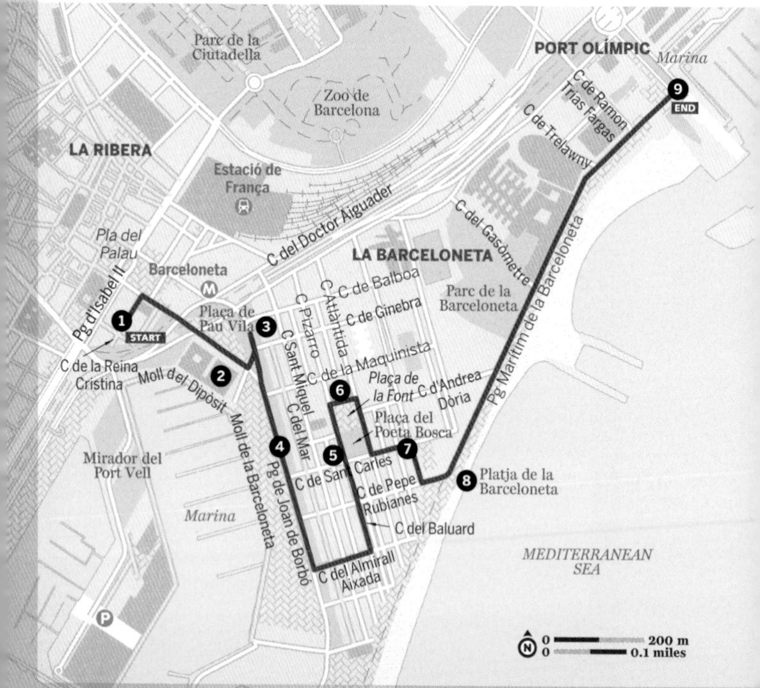

❶ The Cava Crowd

Welcome to Barcelona as it once was. It doesn't come any more authentic than **Can Paixano** (p103), one of the best old-style *cava* (sparkling wine) bars in Barcelona. This ageless bar serves up the pink stuff in elegant little glasses, provided you can elbow your way through the crowds to order.

❷ Seaside Views

Head up to the top floor of the Museu d'Història de Catalunya (you don't need to buy a ticket) to the elegant seafood restaurant **1881** (www.gruposagardi.com/restaurante/1881-per-sagardi; Plaça de Pau Vila 3; mains €19-29; kitchen 10am-midnight Sun-Thu, to 1am Fri & Sat, bar to 1am Sun-Thu, to 3am Fri & Sat;). Step out onto the terrace for a lovely view of the marina.

❸ Beer & Prawns

If you like buzzing, overflowing bars, high-speed staff ready with a smile, a cornucopia of tapas and the illusion that Barcelona hasn't changed in decades, come to **Vaso de Oro** (p101). This place has ice-cold draught beer and the tapas are delicious (try the grilled prawns).

❹ A Waterfront Stroll

Maybe it's a good thing the metro doesn't reach the beach at Barceloneta, obliging you to walk down the sunny portside promenade of **Passeig de Joan de Borbó**. Megayachts sway gently on your right as you bowl down a street crackling with activity.

❺ Mouth-Watering Tapas

There's no sign and the setting is downmarket, but tiny **La Cova Fumada** (p101) always packs in a crowd. The secret? Mouth-watering small plates cooked to perfection in the tiny open kitchen.

❻ Market Buzz

Set in a modern glass and steel building in the heart of the neighbourhood, the **Mercat de la Barceloneta** (www.mercatdelabarceloneta.com; 7am-2pm Mon-Thu & Sat, to 8pm Fri, to 3pm Sun) has the usual array of fresh veg and seafood stalls, as well as the good sit-down restaurant El Guindilla. Across the street, don't miss Baluard Barceloneta, one of the city's best bakeries.

❼ Iconic Drinking Den

Bar Leo (Carrer de Sant Carles 34; noon-9.30pm) is a hole-in-the-wall drinking spot plastered with images of late Andalucian singer and heart-throb Bambino, with a mostly flamenco jukebox. For a youthful, almost entirely *barcelonin* crowd, Bar Leo is it!

❽ Barcelona's Beaches

There are prettier beaches elsewhere on earth, but none so handy for the world's coolest city. **Platja de la Barceloneta** (p104), closest to Barceloneta, yields to Platja de Somorrostro, and both are broad and agreeably long sweeps of sand.

❾ An Olympic Port

A 1.25km promenade shadows the waterfront all the way to the restaurant-lined marina of **Port Olímpic**. An eye-catcher on the approach from Barceloneta is Frank Gehry's giant copper *Peix (Fish)* sculpture, while just to the north is the enticing Platja de Nova Icària.

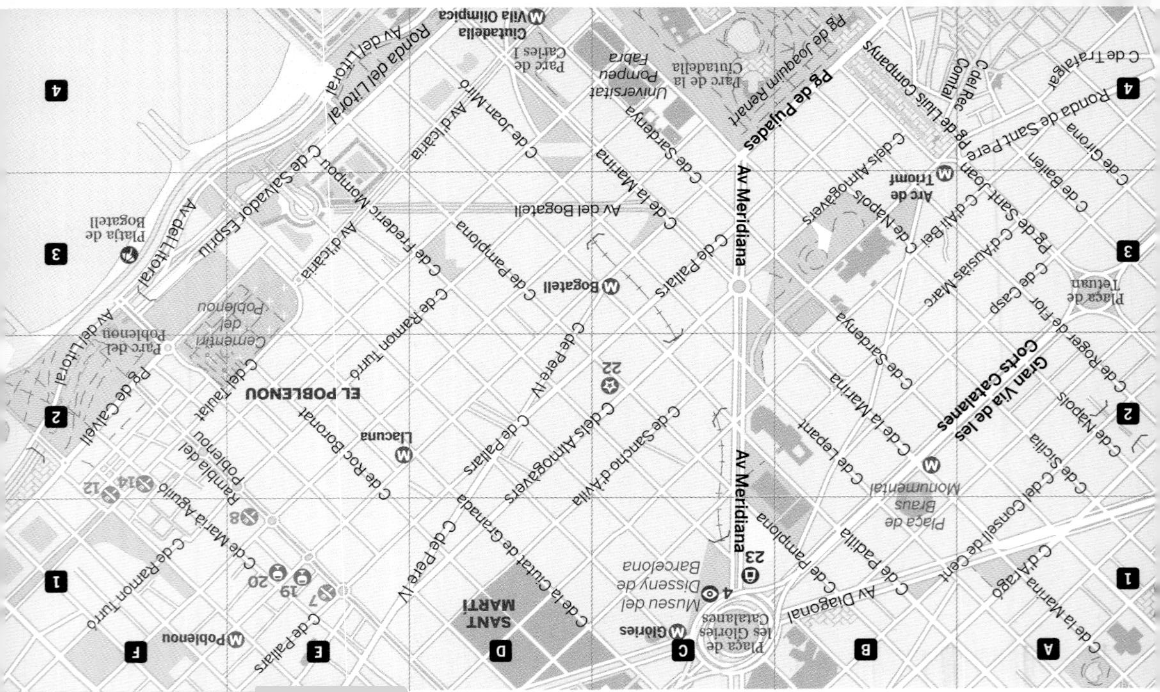

A
B
C
D
E
F
1
2
3
4
Plaça de les Glòries Catalanes
Glòries
Museu del Disseny de Barcelona
4
23
SANT MARTÍ
EL POBLENOU
Poblenou
Llacuna
Bogatell
Ciutadella Vila Olímpica
Arc de Triomf
Av Meridiana
Av Diagonal
Gran Via de les Corts Catalanes
Pg de Pujades
Pg de Lluís Companys
Pg de Joaquim Renart
Pg de Sant Joan
Pg de Calvell
Ronda del Litoral
Ronda de Sant Pere
Av del Litoral
Av del Bogatell
Av d'Icària
C de Salvador Espriu
C de Frederic Mompou
C de Joan Miró
C de Pamplona
C de la Marina
C de Sardenya
C de Pallars
C de Pere IV
C dels Almogàvers
C de Sancho d'Àvila
C de la Ciutat de Granada
C de Ramon Turró
C de Roc Boronat
C de Maria Aguiló
C del Taulat
Rambla del Poblenou
C de Lepant
C de Padilla
C de Nàpols
C de Sicília
C del Consell de Cent
C d'Aragó
C d'Alí Bei
C d'Ausiàs Marc
C de Casp
C de Roger de Flor
C de Bailèn
C de Girona
C de Trafalgar
C del Rec Comtal
Plaça de Tetuan
Plaça de Braus Monumental
Parc de la Ciutadella
Universitat Pompeu Fabra
Parc de Carles I
Parc del Poblenou
Cementiri del Poblenou
Platja de Bogatell
7
8
12
14
19
20
22

Barceloneta & the Beaches

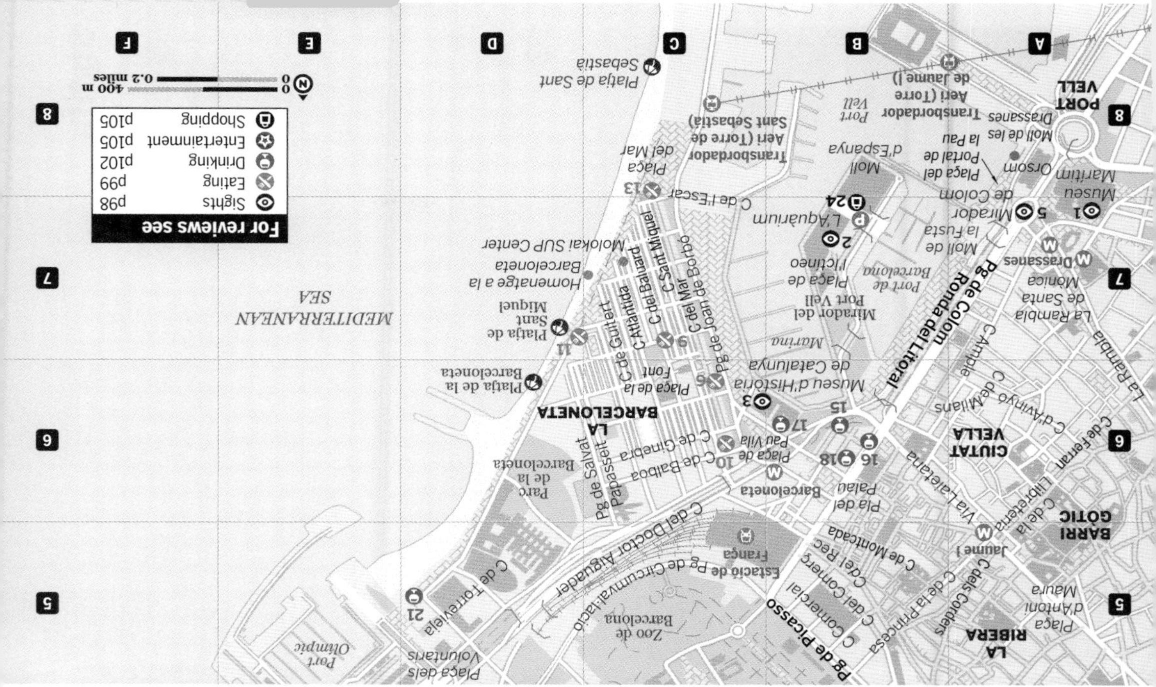

Sights

Museu Marítim MUSEUM

1 MAP P96, A7

The city's maritime museum occupies Gothic shipyards – a remarkable relic from Barcelona's days as the seat of a seafaring empire. Highlights include a full-scale replica of Don Juan of Austria's 16th-century flagship, fishing vessels, antique navigation charts and dioramas of the Barcelona waterfront. (☎93 342 99 20; www.mmb.cat; Avinguda de les Drassanes; adult/child €10/5, free from 3pm Sun; 10am-8pm; M Drassanes)

L'Aquàrium AQUARIUM

2 MAP P96, B7

It's hard not to shudder at the sight of a shark gliding above you, displaying its toothy, wide-mouthed grin. But this, the 80m shark tunnel, is the highlight of one of Europe's largest aquariums. It has the world's best Mediterranean collection and plenty of colourful fish from as far off as the Red Sea, the Caribbean and the Great Barrier Reef. All up, some 11,000 creatures (including a dozen sharks) of 450 species reside here. Tickets are €2 cheaper online. (☎93 221 74 74; www.aquariumbcn.com; Moll d'Espanya; adult/child €20/15, dive €300, Sleeping with Sharks €90; 10am-9.30pm Jul & Aug, shorter hours Sep-Jun; M Drassanes)

Museu d'Història de Catalunya MUSEUM

3 MAP P96, C6

Inside the **Palau de Mar**, this worthwhile museum takes you

Museu del Disseny de Barcelona (p99)

from the Stone Age through to the early 1980s. It's a busy hotchpotch of dioramas, artefacts, videos, models, documents and interactive bits: all up, an entertaining exploration of 2000 years of Catalan history. Signage is in Catalan and Spanish. (Museum of the History of Catalonia; 93 225 47 00; www.mhcat.cat; Plaça de Pau Vila 3; adult/child €4.50/3.50, last Tue of the month Oct-Jun free; 10am-7pm Tue & Thu-Sat, to 8pm Wed, to 2.30pm Sun; M Barceloneta)

Museu del Disseny de Barcelona

MUSEUM

4 MAP P96, C1

Barcelona's design museum lies inside a monolithic contemporary building with geometric facades and a rather brutalist appearance that's nicknamed *la grapadora* (the stapler) by locals. Inside, it houses a dazzling collection of ceramics, decorative arts and textiles, and is a must for anyone interested in the design world. (93 256 68 00; www.museudeldisseny.cat; Plaça de les Glòries Catalanes 37; permanent/temporary exhibition adult €6/4.50, child €4/3, combination ticket adult/child €8/5.50, free from 3pm Sun & 1st Sun of the month; 10am-8pm Tue-Sun; M Glòries)

Mirador de Colom

VIEWPOINT

5 MAP P96, A7

High above the swirl of traffic on the roundabout below, Columbus keeps permanent watch, pointing vaguely out to the Mediterranean from this Corinthian-style iron column built for the 1888 Universal Exhibition. Zip up 60m in a lift for bird's-eye views back up La Rambla and across Barcelona's ports. (Columbus Monument; 93 285 38 32; www.barcelonaturisme.com; Plaça del Portal de la Pau; adult/child €6/4; 8.30am-8.30pm; M Drassanes)

Eating

La Barra de Carles Abellán

SEAFOOD €€€

6 MAP P96, C6

Catalan chef Carles Abellán's stunning glass-encased, glossy-tiled restaurant celebrates seafood in tapas such as pickled octopus, mini anchovy omelettes and fried oyster with salmon roe. Even more show-stopping are the mains: grilled razor clams with *ponzu* citrus sauce, squid filled with spicy poached egg yolk, stir-fried sea cucumber, and lush lobster paella with smoked prawns. (93 760 51 29; www.carlesabellan.com/mis-restaurantes/la-barra; Passeig Joan de Borbó 19; tapas €5-8.50, mains €24-36; 1.30-4pm & 8-11pm; M Barceloneta)

Can Recasens

CATALAN €€

7 MAP P96, E1

One of El Poblenou's most romantic settings, Can Recasens hides a warren of warmly lit rooms full of oil paintings, flickering candles, fairy lights and baskets of fruit. The food is outstanding, with a mix of salads, smoked meats, fondues, and open sandwiches topped with

The Changing Fortunes of Catalonia

Catalan identity is a multifaceted phenomenon, but Catalans are, more than anything else, united by the collective triumphs and shared grievances of the region's tumultuous past.

The Catalan golden age began in the early 12th century when Ramon Berenguer III, who already controlled Catalonia and parts of southern France, launched the region's first seagoing fleet. In 1137 his successor, Ramon Berenguer IV, was betrothed to the one-year-old heiress to the Aragonese throne, thereby giving Catalonia sufficient power to expand its empire out into the Mediterranean. By the end of the 13th century, Catalan rule extended to the Balearic Islands and Catalonia's seaborne trade brought fabulous riches.

But storm clouds were gathering; weakened by a decline in trade and foreign battles, Catalonia was vulnerable. And when Fernando became king of Aragón in 1479 and married Isabel, Queen of Castile, Catalonia became a province of Castile. Catalonia resented its new subordinate status but could do little to overturn it. After backing the losing side in the War of the Spanish Succession (1702–13), Barcelona rose up against the Spanish crown whose armies besieged the city from March 1713 until 11 September 1714. The victorious Felipe V abolished Catalan self-rule, built a huge fort (the Ciutadella) to watch over the city, banned writing and teaching in the Catalan language, and farmed out Catalonia's colonies to other European powers.

Trade again flourished from Barcelona in the following centuries, and by the late 19th and early 20th centuries there were growing calls for greater self-governance to go with the city's burgeoning economic power. However, after Spanish general Francisco Franco's victory in 1939, Catalan Francoists and the dictator's army shot in purges at least 35,000 people, most of whom were either anti-Franco or presumed to be so. Over time, the use of Catalan in public was banned, all street and town names were changed into Spanish, and Castellano Spanish was the only permitted language in schools and the media. Franco's lieutenants remained in control of the city until his death in 1975 and the sense of grievance in Barcelona remains – though today it's directed against the central government in Madrid. Pride in Catalan culture has never been greater, with talk of independence dominating the airwaves throughout Barcelona and the rest of Catalonia.

delicacies like wild mushrooms and Brie, *escalivada* (grilled vegetables) and Gruyère, and spicy chorizo. (93 300 81 23; www.facebook.com/canrecasens; Rambla del Poblenou 102; mains €8-21; 8.30am-1.30pm & 5-11.45pm Mon, to 1am Tue-Thu, to 3am Fri, 9am-1pm & 9pm-3am Sat, 9pm-1am Sun; M Poblenou)

El 58

TAPAS €

8 MAP P96, E1

This French-Catalan place serves imaginative, beautifully prepared tapas dishes: codfish balls with romesco sauce, scallop ceviche, *tartiflette* (cheese, ham and potato casserole), salmon tartare. Solo diners can take a seat at the marble-topped front bar. The back dining room with its exposed brick walls, industrial light fixtures and local artworks is a lively place to linger over a long meal. (Le cinquante huit; Rambla del Poblenou 58; tapas €3.50-12; 1.30-11pm Tue-Sat, to 4pm Sun; M Llacuna)

La Cova Fumada

TAPAS €

9 MAP P96, C7

There's no sign and the setting is decidedly downmarket, but this tiny, buzzing family-run tapas spot always packs in a crowd. The secret? Mouthwatering *pulpo* (octopus), calamari, sardines, *bombas* (meat and potato croquettes served with aioli) and grilled *carxofes* (artichokes) cooked in the open kitchen. Everything is amazingly fresh. (93 221 40 61; Carrer del Baluard 56; tapas €4-12; 9am-3.15pm Mon-Wed, 9am-3.15pm & 6-8.15pm Thu & Fri, 9am-1pm Sat; M Barceloneta)

Vaso de Oro

TAPAS €

10 MAP P96, C6

Always packed, this narrow bar gathers a high-spirited crowd who come for fantastic tapas. Wisecracking, white-jacketed waiters serve plates of grilled *gambes* (prawns), *foie a la plancha* (grilled liver pâté) or *solomillo* (sirloin) chunks. Want something a little different to drink? Ask for a *flauta cincuenta* – half lager and half dark beer. (93 319 30 98; www.vasodeoro.com; Carrer de Balboa 6; tapas €4-12; 11am-midnight; M Barceloneta)

Barraca

SEAFOOD €€

11 MAP P96, D7

Opening to an elevated terrace, this buzzing space has mesmerising views over the Mediterranean – a key reference point in the all-organic dishes served here. Start off with a cauldron of chilli-infused clams, cockles and mussels before moving on to the lavish rice dishes. Vegetarian options are plentiful and it's one of the few places in Barcelona serving a vegan paella. (93 224 12 53; www.tribuwoki.com; Passeig Marítim de la Barceloneta 1; mains €16-22; 12.30-11pm; ; M Barceloneta)

Meet You at the Cubes

German artist Rebecca Horn's elegant **Homenatge a la Barceloneta** (*Homage to Barceloneta*; Map p96, C7; Passeig Marítim; M Barceloneta) sculpture was commissioned for the 1992 Olympics and commemorates the old-fashioned shacks that once lined the beach. Popularly known as 'The Cubes', it's the time-honoured seaside meeting place.

Els Pescadors

SEAFOOD **€€€**

12 MAP P96, F2

On a picturesque square lined with low houses and long-established South American *bella ombre* trees, this quaint family restaurant continues to serve some of the city's best grilled fish and seafood-and-rice dishes. There are three dining areas inside: two are quite modern, while the main room preserves its old tavern flavour. On warm nights, try for a table outside. (93 225 20 18; www.elspescadors.com; Plaça de Prim 1; mains €18-42; 1-3.45pm & 8-11.30pm; ; M Poblenou)

Kaiku

SEAFOOD **€€**

13 MAP P96, C8

Overlooking the waterfront at the south end of Barceloneta, Kaiku incorporates ingredients from the nearby fish market in dishes such as crayfish with mint, swordfish carpaccio with avocado and sun-dried tomatoes, chilli-smeared tuna with green apples and mushrooms, and rice dishes for two. (93 221 90 82; www.restaurantkaiku.cat; Plaça del Mar 1; mains €13-19; 1-3.30pm & 7-10.30pm Tue-Sat, 1-3.30pm Sun; M Barceloneta)

Cal Cuc

ASIAN **€**

14 MAP P96, F2

At this sleek spot, Asian street-food-inspired tapas such as Chinese-inspired bang bang aubergine (in spicy sauce), *gyoza* (Japanese pan-fried dumplings), kimchi (Korean fermented cabbage), tofu *larb* (Laotian marinated tofu) and *takoyaki* (Japanese battered octopus) pair with craft beers from local brewers including BeerCat, Guineu and Les Clandestines. (93 000 28 37; www.mosquitotapas.com/calcuc; Carrer del Taulat 109; tapas €4-8; 6pm-midnight Mon-Thu, 1pm-1am Fri-Sun; ; M Poblenou)

Drinking

Perikete

WINE BAR

15 MAP P96, B6

Since opening in 2017, this fabulous wine bar has been jam-packed with locals. Hams hang from the ceilings, barrels of vermouth sit above the bar and wine bottles cram every available shelf space – over 200 varieties are available by the glass or bottle, accompanied by 50-plus tapas dishes. In the evening, the action spills into the street. (www.gruporeini.net/perikete;

Carrer de Llauder 6; ⌚11am-1am; Ⓜ Barceloneta)

Bodega Vidrios y Cristales

WINE BAR

16 MAP P96, B6

In a history-steeped, stone-floored building dating from 1840, this atmospheric little jewel recreates a neighbourhood bodega with tins of sardines, anchovies and other delicacies lining the shelves (used in exquisite tapas dishes), house-made vermouth, and a wonderful array of wines. Be prepared to stand as there are no seats (a handful of upturned wine barrels let you rest your glass). (www.gruposagardi.com/restaurante/bodega-vidrios-y-cristales; Passeig d'Isabel II 6; ⌚noon-midnight Sun-Thu, to 1am Fri & Sat; Ⓜ Barceloneta)

BlackLab

MICROBREWERY

17 MAP P96, B6

Barcelona's first brewhouse opened back in 2014 inside the historic Palau de Mar (p98). Its taps feature 18 house-made brews, including saisons, double IPAs and dry stouts, and the brewmasters constantly experiment with new flavours, such as a sour Berliner Weisse with fiery jalapeño. One-hour tours (5pm Sundays; €12) offer a behind-the-scenes look at the brewers in action plus four samples. (☎93 221 83 60; www.blacklab.es; Plaça de Pau Vila 1; ⌚noon-1.30am; Ⓜ Barceloneta)

Can Paixano

WINE BAR

18 MAP P96, B6

This lofty *cava* bar (also called La Xampanyeria) has long been run

Exterior of CLDC (p104)

on a winning formula. The standard tipple is bubbly rosé in elegant little glasses, combined with bite-sized *bocadillos* (filled rolls) and tapas. Note that this place is usually packed to the rafters, and elbowing your way to the bar can be a titanic struggle. (☎93 310 08 39; www.canpaixano.com; Carrer de la Reina Cristina 7; ⏱9am-10.30pm Mon-Sat; Ⓜ Barceloneta)

Beach Libraries

In July and August (typically 10am to 5pm Tuesday to Sunday), the city sets up *biblioplatges* ('beach libraries') underneath the boardwalk at the northern end of **Platja de la Barceloneta** (Map p96, D6; http://lameva.barcelona.cat; Ⓜ Barceloneta) – techincally called Platja de Somorrostro – and at **Platja de la Mar Bella** (http://lameva.barcelona.cat; Ⓜ Ciutadella Vila Olímpica, Llacuna, Poblenou, Selva de Mar) at the Espigó de Bac de Roda. You'll find magazines, newspapers and a small foreign-language selection among the Spanish titles.

At the same locations, you can also hire out frisbees, volleyballs and nets, beach rackets, balls and *petanque* games; for the kiddies, you'll find buckets, spades and watering cans. They're free to use; all you need to hire out books or gear is your ID.

Madame George

LOUNGE

19 MAP P96, E1

A theatrical (veering towards campy) elegance marks the interior of this small, chandelier-lit lounge just off the Rambla del Poblenou. Deft bartenders stir well-balanced cocktails like a Lychee-tini (vanilla-infused vodka, fresh lychees, lychee liqueur and lemon juice) in vintage glassware, while a DJ spins vinyl (mainly soul and funk) in the corner. (www.madamegeorgebar.com; Carrer de Pujades 179; ⏱6pm-2am Mon-Thu, to 3am Fri & Sat, to 12.30am Sun; Ⓜ Poblenou)

Balius

COCKTAIL BAR

20 MAP P96, E1

There's an old-fashioned jauntiness to this vintage cocktail den in El Poblenou. Staff pour a mix of classic libations as well as vermouths, and there's a small tapas menu until 10.30pm. Stop by on Sundays to catch live jazz, starting around 7.30pm. (☎93 315 86 50; www.baliusbar.com; Carrer de Pujades 196; ⏱6pm-2am Tue & Wed, 5pm-3am Thu-Sat, to 1am Sun; Ⓜ Poblenou)

CDLC

LOUNGE

21 MAP P96, D5

Ideal for a slow warm-up before heading to the nearby clubs, Carpe Diem Lounge Club has Asian-inspired decor and opens onto the beach. Its Asian-fusion food (sushi et al) is quite good, but pricey; alternatively wait until about midnight, when the tables are rolled up and the DJs and dancers take full control. (Carpe Diem Lounge Club; ☎93 224 04 70; www.cdlcbarcelona.com; Passeig Marítim de la Barceloneta 32; ⏲noon-5am; Ⓜ Ciutadella Vila Olímpica)

Entertainment

Razzmatazz

LIVE MUSIC

22 MAP P96, C2

Bands from far and wide occasionally create scenes of near hysteria in this, one of the city's classic live-music and clubbing venues. Bands can appear throughout the week (check the website), with different start times. On weekends live music later gives way to club sounds. (☎93 320 82 00; www.salarazzmatazz.com; Carrer de Pamplona 88; tickets from €17; ⏲9pm-4am; Ⓜ Bogatell)

Shopping

Els Encants Vells

MARKET

23 MAP P96, C1

In a gleaming open-sided complex near Plaça de les Glòries Catalanes, the 'Old Charms' flea market is the biggest of its kind in Barcelona. Over 500 vendors ply their wares beneath massive mirror-like panels. It's all here, from antique furniture through to secondhand clothes. There's a lot of junk, but you'll occasionally stumble across a *ganga* (bargain). (Fira de Bellcaire; ☎93 246 30 30; www.encantsbcn.com; Plaça de les Glòries Catalanes; ⏲9am-8pm Mon, Wed, Fri & Sat; Ⓜ Glòries)

Adventures on the Waterfront

Molokai SUP Center (☎93 221 48 68; www.molokaisupcenter.com; Carrer de Meer 39; 2hr private lesson €60, SUP rental per hour €15; Ⓜ Barceloneta) Go for a gentle paddle out on the Mediterranean.

Platja de Sant Sebastià (http://lameva.barcelona.cat; Ⓜ Barceloneta) The starting point for a scenic run or cycle along the waterfront.

Orsom (☎93 441 05 37; www.barcelona-orsom.com; Moll de les Drassanes; adult/child €15.50/13.50; ⏲May-early Oct; Ⓜ Drassanes) Watch the sunset on a peaceful sailing cruise.

Maremàgnum

MALL

24 MAP P96, B7

Created out of largely abandoned docks, this buzzing shopping centre, with its 19 places to eat, bars and cinemas, is home to 59 shops including youthful Spanish chain Mango, and eye-catching fashions from Barcelona-based Desigual. Football fans will be drawn to the paraphernalia at FC Botiga. It's particularly popular on Sundays when most other stores in the city remain shuttered. (☎93 225 81 00; www.maremagnum.es; Moll d'Espanya 5; ⏲10am-10pm; Ⓜ Drassanes)

Explore

Passeig de Gràcia & L'Eixample

The elegant, if traffic-filled, district of L'Eixample (pronounced 'lay-sham-pluh') is a showcase for Modernista architecture, including Gaudí's unfinished masterpiece La Sagrada Família. L'Eixample also has a celebrated dining scene, along with high-end boutiques and wildly diverse nightlife. Gilded cocktail lounges and the buzzing gay club scene of 'Gaixample' are all part of the mix.

If you linger over the weird-and-wonderful detail of the Casa Batlló (p114) and La Pedrera (p108), you could easily spend a couple of hours in each, which should just leave time to admire Casa Amatller (p114) and get the low-down on contemporary art at the Fundació Antoni Tàpies. (p114)

Follow up with a tapas feast at Carles Abellan's inventive Tapas 24 (p118), and a walk along elegant Passeig de Gràcia. Finish off the afternoon at the Museu del Modernisme Barcelona (p117).

Perhaps try dinner at Casa Calvet (p119), with its otherwise inaccessible Gaudí interiors. Dry Martini (p121) is a great place to ease into the evening.

Getting There & Around

M Four metro lines criss-cross L'Eixample, three stopping at Passeig de Gràcia for the Illa de la Discòrdia. Línia 3 stops at Diagonal for La Pedrera, while Línies 2 and 5 stop at Sagrada Família.

FGC lines from Plaça de Catalunya take you one stop to Provença, in the heart of L'Eixample.

Neighbourhood Map on p112

Facade of Casa Amatller (p114) MATTEO COZZI/SHUTTERSTOCK ©

Top Sight

La Pedrera

La Pedrera – officially called Casa Milà after its owners, but nicknamed La Pedrera (the Stone Quarry) by bemused locals who watched Gaudí build it from 1905–10 – is in the top tier of Gaudí's achievements. Conceived as an apartment block, its approach to space and to light and its blurring of the dividing line between decoration and functionality are astounding.

MAP P112, D2

Casa Milà

902 202138

www.lapedrera.com

Passeig de Gràcia 92

adult/child €25/15

9am-8.30pm Mar-Oct, 9am-6.30pm Nov-Feb

M Diagonal

The Facade

The natural world was one of the most enduring influences on Gaudí's work, and La Pedrera's undulating grey stone facade evokes a cliff-face sculpted by waves and wind. The wave effect is emphasised by elaborate wrought-iron balconies that bring to mind seaweed washed up on the shore. The lasting impression is of a building on the verge of motion.

The Roof Terrace

Gaudí's blend of mischievous form with ingenious functionality is evident on the roof, with its clusters of chimneys, stairwells and ventilation towers that rise and fall atop the structure's wave-like contours like giant medieval knights. Some are unadorned, others are decorated with *trencadís* (ceramic fragments) and even broken cava bottles. The deep patios, which Gaudí treated like interior facades, flood the apartments with natural light.

Espai Gaudí

With 270 gracious parabolic arches, the Espai Gaudí feels like the fossilised ribcage of some giant prehistoric beast. At one point, 12 arches come together to form a palm tree. Watch out also for the strange optical effect of the mirror and hanging sculpture on the east side.

La Pedrera Apartment

Below the attic, the apartment (El Pis de la Pedrera) spreads out. Bathed in evenly distributed light, twisting and turning with the building's rippling distribution, the labyrinthine apartment is Gaudí's vision of domestic bliss. In the ultimate nod to flexible living, the apartment has no load-bearing walls: the interior walls could thus be moved to suit the inhabitants' needs.

★ Top Tips

- La Pedrera is extremely popular: buy tickets online and arrive at opening time to avoid the worst of the crowds.
- A 'Premium' ticket (adult/child €29/11) means you don't have to queue. Other queue-free options include a 'day and night' ticket (€41/23.50).
- Guided evening tours (€44/23.50) show the mysterious side of La Pedrera. Reserve a spot in advance.
- On Fridays and Saturday evenings from early June to early September, La Pedrera hosts open-air concerts on the roof (€30 including a tour and a drink).

Take a Break

A 300m walk southwest of La Pedrera, La Bodegueta Provença (p120) is a classy spot serving first-rate tapas and wines by the glass.

An excellent choice any time (coffee and croissants, or tapas for lunch or dinner), Cerveseria Catalana (p120) is 400m south near the Rambla de Catalunya.

Walking Tour

Shop in the Quadrat d'Or

While visitors to L'Eixample do the sights, locals go shopping in the Quadrat d'Or (Golden Square), the grid of streets either side of Passeig de Gràcia. This is Barcelona at its most fashion- and design-conscious, which also describes a large proportion of L'Eixample's residents. All the big names are here, alongside boutiques of local designers who capture the essence of Barcelona cool.

Walk Facts

Start Lurdes Bergada

End Cosmo

Length 1.6km; 3–5 hours

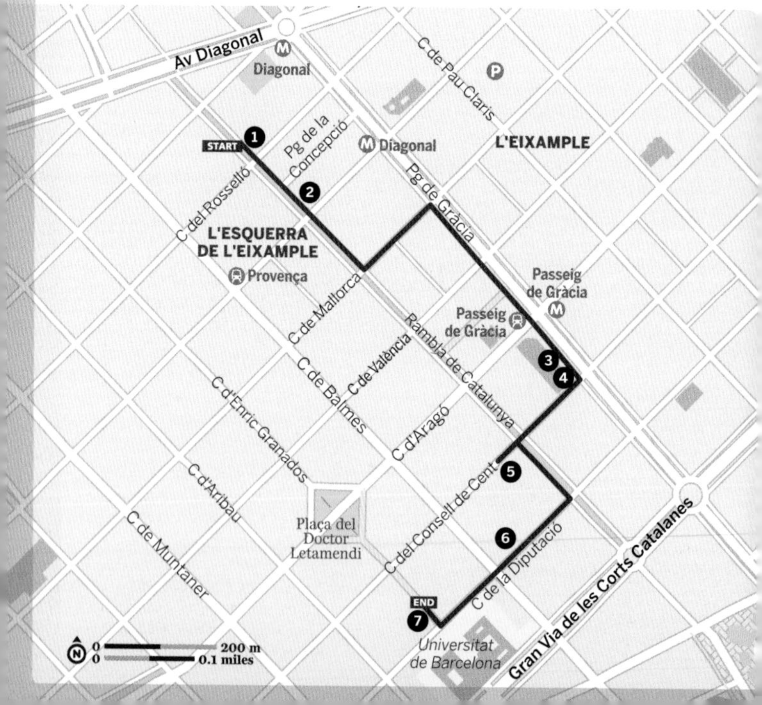

❶ The New Wave

You could spend an entire day along Passeig de Gràcia but detour for a moment to **Lurdes Bergada** (☎93 218 48 51; www.lurdesbergada.es; Rambla de Catalunya 112; ⏰10.30am-8.30pm Mon-Sat), a boutique run by mother-and-son designer team Lurdes Bergada and Syngman Cucala. The classy men's and women's fashions use natural fibres and have attracted a cult following.

❷ The Sweet Life

Time for a break. And few pastry shops have such a long-established pedigree as **Mauri** (☎93 215 10 20; www.pasteleriasmauri.com; Rambla de Catalunya 102; pastries €3.50-6.50; ⏰8am-midnight Mon-Fri, 9am-10pm Sat, 9am-4.30pm Sun). The plush interior is capped by an ornate fresco dating back to Mauri's first days in 1929. Its croissants and featherlight *ensaïmadas* (sweet buns) are near perfect.

❸ Modernista Jewellery

This is more than just any old jewellery store. The boys from **Bagués-Masriera** (p123) have been chipping away at precious stones and moulding metal since the 19th century, and many of the classic pieces here have a flighty, Modernista influence. Bagués backs it up with service that can be haughty, but owes much to old-school courtesies.

❹ Luxury Luggage

While bags and suitcases in every conceivable colour of buttersoft leather are the mainstay at **Loewe** (☎93 216 04 00; www.loewe.com; Passeig de Gràcia 35; ⏰10am-8.30pm Mon-Sat), there is also a range of clothing for men and women, along with some stunning – and stunningly priced – accessories. The shop itself is worth a visit, housed in the **Casa Lleó Morera** (p115), and with some interior details by Domènech i Montaner.

❺ Say It with Chocolate

A sleek and modern temple to the brown stuff, **Cacao Sampaka** (☎93 272 08 33; www.cacaosampaka.com; Carrer del Consell de Cent 292; ⏰9am-9pm Mon-Sat) doubles as a shop and cafe and is the perfect place to stock up with gifts to take back home. Select from every conceivable flavour (rosemary, anyone, or curry?), either in bar form or as individual choccies to fill your own elegant little gift box.

❻ Fine Wines

For superior souvenirs in liquid form, head to the state-of-the-art **Monvínic** (p120), a veritable palace of wine with more than 3000 wines in its cellar, including some extremely rare finds. Try before you buy in the wine bar, and ask them to make you up a gift box for someone special back home.

❼ Chill Down

Cosmo (☎93 105 79 92; www.galeriacosmo.com; Carrer d'Enric Granados 3; ⏰10am-10pm) is a bright, white cavernous space, dotted with colour from the exhibitions that adorn its high walls. It has a nice selection of teas, cakes and snacks. Set on a pleasant pedestrian strip, it's perfect for an evening tipple outside or in.

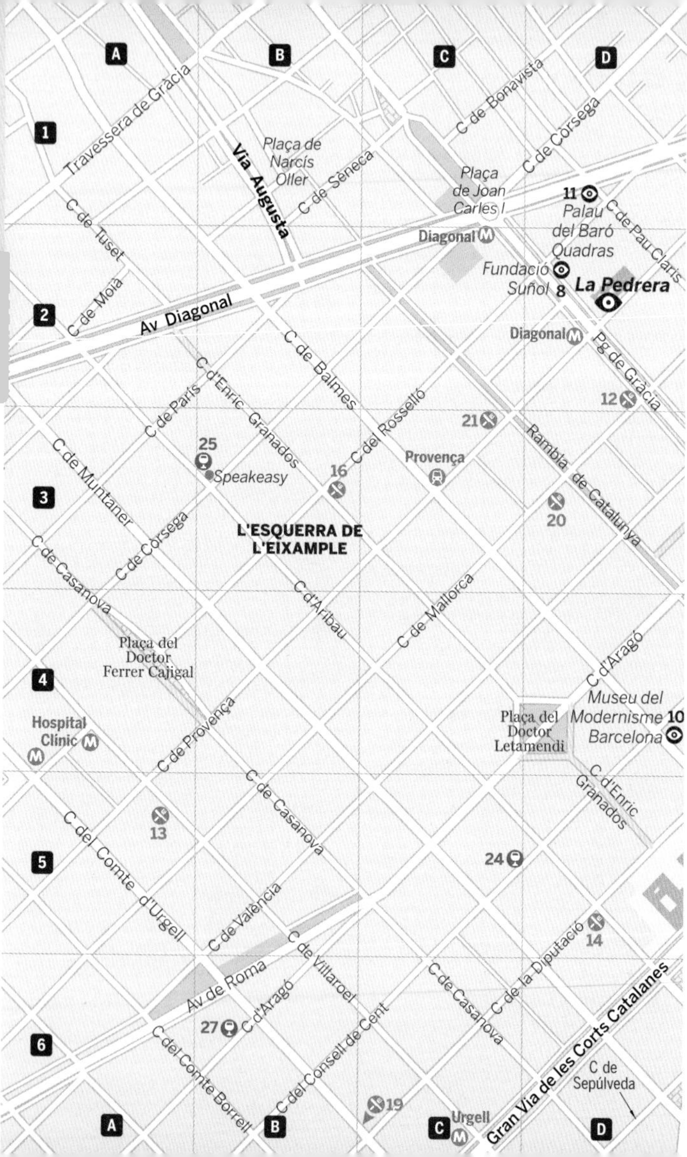
A
B
C
D
1
2
3
4
5
6
Travessera de Gràcia
C de Bonavista
C de Còrsega
Plaça de Narcís Oller
Via Augusta
C de Sèneca
Plaça de Joan Carles I
11
Palau del Baró Quadras
C de Pau Claris
C de Tuset
Diagonal
Fundació Suñol 8
La Pedrera
C de Moià
Av Diagonal
Diagonal
Pg de Gràcia
C de Balmes
C d'Enric Granados
C de París
12
21
C del Rosselló
Rambla de Catalunya
25
Speakeasy
16
Provença
C de Muntaner
20
C de Còrsega
L'ESQUERRA DE L'EIXAMPLE
C de Casanova
C d'Aribau
C de Mallorca
Plaça del Doctor Ferrer Cajigal
C d'Aragó
Museu del Modernisme Barcelona 10
Hospital Clínic
Plaça del Doctor Letamendi
C de Provença
C d'Enric Granados
C de Casanova
13
C del Comte d'Urgell
24
C de València
14
C de Villaroel
C de la Diputació
Av de Roma
C de Casanova
Gran Via de les Corts Catalanes
27
C d'Aragó
C del Consell de Cent
C del Comte Borrell
C de Sepúlveda
19
Urgell

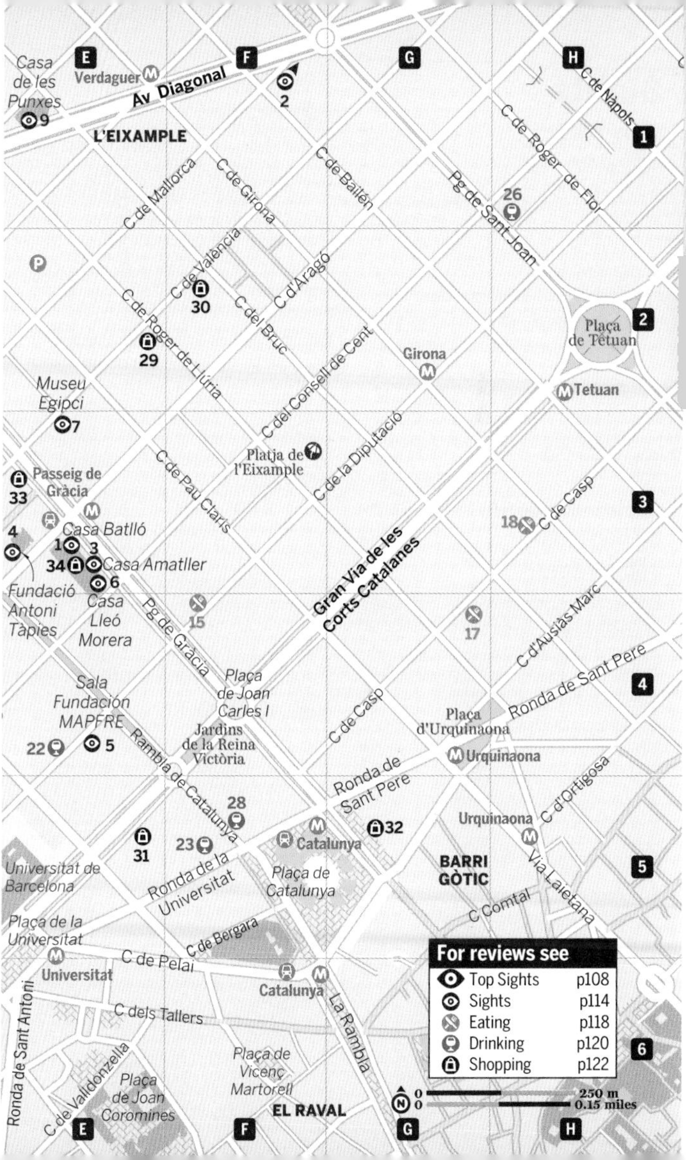
E
F
G
H
1
2
3
4
5
6
Casa de les Punxes
9
Verdaguer
Av Diagonal
2
L'EIXAMPLE
C de Nàpols
C de Roger de Flor
C de Mallorca
C de Girona
C de Bailén
Pg de Sant Joan
26
C de València
30
C d'Aragó
C del Bruc
C de Roger de Llúria
29
Plaça de Tetuan
Girona
Tetuan
C del Consell de Cent
Museu Egipci
7
C de la Diputació
Platja de l'Eixample
Passeig de Gràcia
33
C de Pau Claris
C de Casp
18
Casa Batlló
4
1
3
34
Casa Amatller
6
Fundació Antoni Tàpies
Casa Lleó Morera
Gran Via de les Corts Catalanes
15
17
Pg de Gràcia
C d'Ausiàs Marc
Ronda de Sant Pere
Sala Fundación MAPFRE
Plaça de Joan Carles I
Jardins de la Reina Victòria
C de Casp
Plaça d'Urquinaona
22
5
Urquinaona
Rambla de Catalunya
Ronda de Sant Pere
C d'Ortigosa
28
32
Urquinaona
31
23
Catalunya
Universitat de Barcelona
Ronda de la Universitat
Plaça de Catalunya
BARRI GÒTIC
Via Laietana
C Comtal
Plaça de la Universitat
C de Bergara
Universitat
C de Pelai
Catalunya
C dels Tallers
La Rambla
Ronda de Sant Antoni
C de Valldonzella
Plaça de Joan Coromines
Plaça de Vicenç Martorell
EL RAVAL
For reviews see
Top Sights p108
Sights p114
Eating p118
Drinking p120
Shopping p122
0 250 m
0 0.15 miles

Sights

Casa Batlló ARCHITECTURE

1 MAP P112, E3

One of the strangest residential buildings in Europe, this is Gaudí at his hallucinatory best. The facade, sprinkled with bits of blue, mauve and green tiles and studded with wave-shaped window frames and balconies, rises to an uneven blue-tiled roof with a solitary tower. (93 216 03 06; www.casabatllo.es; Passeig de Gràcia 43; adult/child €28/free; 9am-9pm, last admission 8pm; M Passeig de Gràcia)

Recinte Modernista de Sant Pau ARCHITECTURE

2 MAP P112, F1

Domènech i Montaner outdid himself as architect and philanthropist with the Modernista Hospital de la Santa Creu i de Sant Pau, renamed the 'Recinte Modernista' in 2014. It was long considered one of the city's most important hospitals but was repurposed, its various spaces becoming cultural centres, offices and something of a monument. The complex, including 16 pavilions – together with the Palau de la Música Catalana (p84), a joint Unesco World Heritage Site – is lavishly decorated and each pavilion is unique. (93 553 78 01; www.santpaubarcelona.org; Carrer de Sant Antoni Maria Claret 167; adult/child €13/free; 9.30am-6.30pm Mon-Sat, to 2.30pm Sun Apr-Oct, 9.30am-4.30pm Mon-Sat, to 2.30pm Sun Nov-Mar; M Sant Pau/Dos de Maig)

Casa Amatller ARCHITECTURE

3 MAP P112, E3

One of Puig i Cadafalch's most striking flights of Modernista fantasy, Casa Amatller combines Gothic window frames with a stepped gable borrowed from Dutch urban architecture. But the busts and reliefs of dragons, knights and other characters dripping off the main facade are pure caprice.The pillared foyer and staircase lit by stained glass are like the inside of some romantic castle. The building was renovated in 1900 for the chocolate baron and philanthropist Antoni Amatller (1851–1910). (93 461 74 60; www.amatller.org; Passeig de Gràcia 41; adult/child 1hr guided tour €17/8.50, 40min multimedia tour €14/7, with 20min chocolate tasting €17/10; 11am-6pm; M Passeig de Gràcia)

Fundació Antoni Tàpies GALLERY

4 MAP P112, E3

The Fundació Antoni Tàpies is both a pioneering Modernista building (completed in 1885) and the major collection of leading 20th-century Catalan artist Antoni Tàpies. Tàpies died in February 2012, aged 88; known for his esoteric work, he left behind a powerful range of paintings and a foundation intended to promote contemporary artists. Admission includes an audioguide. (93 487 03 15; www.fundaciotapies.org; Carrer d'Aragó 255; adult/child €7/5.60; 10am-7pm Tue-Sun; M Passeig de Gràcia)

Sala Fundación MAPFRE

GALLERY

5 MAP P112, E4

Formerly the Fundación Francisco Godia, this stunning, carefully restored Modernista residence was taken over in late 2015 by the charitable cultural arm of Spanish insurance giants MAPFRE as a space for art and photography exhibitions. Housed in the Casa Garriga i Nogués, it is a stunning, carefully restored Modernista residence originally built for a rich banking family by Enric Sagnier in 1902–05. (93 401 26 03; www.fundacionmapfre.org; Carrer de la Diputació 250; adult/child €3/free, Mon free; 2-8pm Mon, 10am-8pm Tue-Sat, 11am-7pm Sun; M Passeig de Gràcia)

Casa Lleó Morera

ARCHITECTURE

6 MAP P112, E3

Domènech i Montaner's 1905 contribution to the Illa de la Discòrdia, with Modernista carving outside and a bright, tiled lobby in which floral motifs predominate, is perhaps the least odd-looking of the three main buildings on the block. Luxury fashion store Loewe (p111) is located here. (Passeig de Gràcia 35; M Passeig de Gràcia)

Museu Egipci

MUSEUM

7 MAP P112, E3

Hotel magnate Jordi Clos has spent much of his life collecting ancient Egyptian artefacts, brought together in this private museum. It's divided into different thematic areas (the pharaoh, religion, funerary practices, mummification, crafts etc)

Facade of Casa Lleó Morera

Modernisme

In the late 19th century, Barcelona was booming and the city's culture of avant-garde experimentation was custom made for a group of outrageously talented architects who came to be known as Modernistas. Leading the way was Antoni Gaudí i Cornet (1852–1926). Gaudí personifies and largely transcends a movement that brought a thunderclap of innovative greatness to an otherwise middle-ranking European city.

The Style

Modernisme did not appear in isolation in Barcelona. To the British and French the style was art nouveau; the Germans called it Jugendstil (Youth Style). Whatever it was called, a key uniting element was the sensuous curve, implying movement, lightness and vitality. Modernista architects looked to the past for inspiration: Gothic, Islamic and Renaissance design in particular. At its most playful, Modernisme was able to intelligently flout the rule books of these styles and create exciting new cocktails.

The Architects

Gaudí and the two architects who most closely followed him in talent, Lluís Domènech i Montaner (1850–1923) and Josep Puig i Cadafalch (1867–1957), were Catalan nationalists. The political associations are significant, as Modernisme became a means of expression for Catalan identity; the style barely touched the rest of Spain. Gaudí took great inspiration from Gothic styles, but he also sought to emulate the harmony he observed in nature. Straight lines were out. The forms of plants and stones were in. Gaudí used complex string models weighted with plumb lines to make his calculations. The architect's work is at once a sublime reaching out to the heavens, and an earthy appeal to sinewy movement.

The Materials & Decoration

Stone, unclad brick, exposed iron and steel frames, and copious use of stained glass and ceramics in decoration, were all features of the new style. Modernista architects relied heavily on the skills of craftsmen who were the heirs of the guild masters and had absorbed centuries of knowhow about working with these materials. There were no concrete pours. Gaudí in particular relied on the old skills and even ran schools in La Sagrada Família workshops in a bid to keep them alive. Newer materials, such as forged iron, also came into their own during this period.

and boasts an interesting variety of exhibits. (☎93 488 01 88; www.museuegipci.com; Carrer de València 284; adult/child €11/5; ⏲10am-8pm Mon-Sat, to 2pm Sun mid-Jun–early Oct & Dec, 10am-2pm & 4-8pm Mon-Fri, 10am-8pm Sat, 10am-2pm Sun Jan–mid-Jun & early Oct-Nov; M Passeig de Gràcia)

Fundació Suñol GALLERY

8 MAP P112, D2

Rotating exhibitions of portions of this private collection of mostly 20th-century art (some 1200 works in total) offer anything from Man Ray's photography to sculptures by Alberto Giacometti. Over two floors, you are most likely to run into Spanish artists – anyone from Picasso to Jaume Plensa – along with a sprinkling of international artists.

It makes a refreshing pause between the crush of crowded Modernista monuments on this boulevard. Indeed, you get an interesting side view of one of them, La Pedrera (p108), from out the back. (☎93 496 10 32; www.fundaciosunol.org; Passeig de Gràcia 98; adult/child €4/free; ⏲11am-2pm & 4-8pm Mon-Fri, 4-8pm Sat; M Diagonal)

Casa de les Punxes ARCHITECTURE

9 MAP P112, E1

Puig i Cadafalch's Casa Terrades, completed in 1905, is better known as the Casa de les Punxes (House of Spikes) because of its pointed turrets. Resembling a medieval castle, the former apartment block is the only fully detached building in L'Eixample, and was declared a national monument in 1976. Since 2017 it has been open to the public. Visits take in its stained-glass bay windows, handsome iron staircase, and rooftop. Guided tours in English lasting one hour depart at 4pm. (Casa Terrades; ☎93 016 01 28; www.casadelespunxes.com; Avinguda Diagonal 420; adult/child audiogude tour €12.50/11.25, guided tour €20/17; ⏲9am-8pm; M Diagonal)

Museu del Modernisme Barcelona MUSEUM

10 MAP P112, D4

Housed in a Modernista building, this museum's ground floor seems like a big Modernista furniture showroom. Several items by Antoni Gaudí, including chairs from Casa Batlló and a mirror from Casa Calvet, are supplemented by a host of items by his lesser-known contemporaries, including some typically whimsical, mock medieval pieces by Puig i Cadafalch. (☎93 272 28 96; www.mmbcn.cat; Carrer de Balmes 48; adult/child €10/5; ⏲10.30am-7pm Tue-Sat, to 2pm Sun; M Passeig de Gràcia)

Palau del Baró Quadras ARCHITECTURE

11 MAP P112, D1

Puig i Cadafalch designed Palau del Baró Quadras (built 1902–06) in an exuberant Gothic-inspired style. The main facade is its most intriguing, with a soaring, glassed-in gallery. Take a closer look at the gargoyles and reliefs – the pair of toothy fish and the sword-wielding knight clearly have the same artistic

Platja de L'Eixample

In a hidden garden inside a typical Eixample block is an old water tower and an urban 'beach', the **Platja de l'Eixample** (Map p112, F3; 93 423 43 50; Carrer de Roger de Llúria 56; €1.55; 10am-8pm late Jun–Sep; M Girona). In reality, this is a knee-height swimming pool (60cm at its deepest) surrounded by sand. It's perfect for little ones, with lifeguards on hand.

signature as the architect behind Casa Amatller. The only way to visit the interior is on a 45-minute tour; English tours depart on Wednesday at 11am. (93 467 80 00; www.llull.cat; Avinguda Diagonal 373; tour adult/child €10/free; 11am-1pm Wed; M Diagonal)

Eating

Lasarte

MODERN EUROPEAN **€€€**

12 MAP P112, D2

One of the preeminent restaurants in Barcelona – and the city's first to gain three Michelin stars – Lasarte is overseen by lauded chef Martín Berasategui. From Duroc pig's trotters with quince to squid tartare with kaffir consommé, this is seriously sophisticated stuff, served in an ultra-contemporary dining room by waiting staff who could put the most overawed diners at ease. (93 445 32 42; www.restaurantlasarte.com; Carrer de Mallorca 259; mains €52-58; 1.30-3.30pm & 8.30-10.30pm Tue-Sat, closed 1st 3 weeks Aug; M Diagonal)

Disfrutar

MODERN EUROPEAN **€€€**

13 MAP P112, A5

Disfrutar ('Enjoy' in Catalan) is among the city's finest restaurants, with two Michelin stars. Run by alumni of Ferran Adrià's game-changing (now closed) El Bulli restaurant, nothing is as it seems, such as black and green olives that are actually chocolate ganache with orange-blossom water. (93 348 68 96; www.en.disfrutarbarcelona.com; Carrer de Villarroel 163; tasting menus €120-185; 1-2.45pm & 8-9.45pm Tue-Sat; M Hospital Clínic)

Mont Bar

BISTRO **€€€**

14 MAP P112, D5

Named for the owner's Val d'Aran hometown, this stylish wine-bar-style space with black-and-white floors, forest-green banquette and bottle-lined walls offers next-level cooking. Exquisite tapas (pig's trotters with baby shrimp; plankton meringue with sea anemone and Mascarpone) precede 'small plate' mains (tuna belly with pine-nut emulsion) and showstopping desserts (sheep's milk ice cream with blackcurrant liqueur sauce). Reservations essential. (93 323 95 90; www.montbar.com; Carrer de la Diputació 220; tapas €2-13, mains €12.50-26.50; noon-3.30pm & 7pm-midnight; M Universitat)

Tapas 24

TAPAS **€**

15 MAP P112, F4

Hotshot chef Carles Abellán runs this basement tapas haven

known for its gourmet versions of old faves. Highlights include the *bikini* (toasted ham and cheese sandwich – here the ham is cured and the truffle makes all the difference) and zesty *boquerones al limón* (lemon-marinated anchovies). You can't book but it's worth the wait. (93 488 09 77; www.carlesabellan.com; Carrer de la Diputació 269; tapas €2.20-12; 9am-midnight; ; M Passeig de Gràcia)

Auto Rosellon INTERNATIONAL €€

16 MAP P112, B3

With cornflower-blue paintwork and all its fresh produce on display, Auto Rosellon utilises mostly organic ingredients sourced from small producers and its own garden in dishes like eggs Benedict, salmon tartare with avocado, ricotta gnocchi with confit tomatoes and thyme, and slow-roasted pork tacos. Homemade juices and rose lemonade are exceptional; there are also great cocktails and craft beers. (93 853 93 20; www.autorosellon.com; Carrer de Rosselló 182; mains €12-18; 8am-1am Mon-Wed, 8am-2am Thu & Fri, 9am-2am Sat, 9am-midnight Sun; ; FGC Provença)

Casa Calvet CATALAN €€€

17 MAP P112, G4

An early Gaudí masterpiece loaded with his trademark curvy features houses a swish restaurant (just to the right of the building's main entrance). Dress up and ask for an intimate *taula cabina* (wooden booth). You could opt for scallop- and prawn-stuffed artichokes, partridge and chestnut casserole

Montaditos at Cerveseria Catalana (p120)

or veal with duck-liver sauce. (☎93 412 40 12; www.casacalvet.es; Carrer de Casp 48; mains €27-35; ⏰1-3.30pm & 8-10.30pm Mon-Sat; Ⓜ Urquinaona)

Hawker 45 — ASIAN €

18 MAP P112, H3

Taking its cues from an Asian hawkers market, this aromatic spot sizzles up street-food dishes such as spicy Malaysian squid laksa, Indonesian lamb satay, Korean Kalbi pork ribs with rice cakes, Thai crying tiger beef salad and Singaporean green mango sambal with steamed crab. Its six-course tasting menu (€35) is best paired with craft beers (€42) or Asian-inspired cocktails (€60). (☎93 763 83 15; Carrer de Casp 45; mains €8.50-16; ⏰1-4pm & 8-11pm Mon-Fri, 12.30-4pm & 8-11.30pm Sat, 12.30-4pm Sun; Ⓜ Tetuan)

Copasetic — CAFE €

19 MAP P112, C6

Decked out with retro furniture, Copasetic has a fun, friendly vibe. The menu holds plenty for everyone, whether your thing is eggs Benedict, wild-berry tartlets or a fat, juicy burger. There are lots of vegetarian, gluten-free and organic options, and superb (and reasonably priced) weekend brunches. Lunch *menús* (Tuesday to Friday) cost between €9.50 and €12. (☎93 532 76 66; www.copaseticbarcelona.com; Carrer de la Diputació 55; mains €6-13.50; ⏰10.30am-midnight Tue & Wed, to 1am Thu, to 2am Fri & Sat, to 5.30pm Sun; 📶 🌱; Ⓜ Rocafort)

Cerveseria Catalana — TAPAS €€

20 MAP P112, D3

The 'Catalan Brewery' is perfect at all hours: for a morning coffee and croissant, or sangria, *montaditos* (canapés) and tapas at lunch or dinner. You can sit at the bar, on the pavement terrace or in the restaurant at the back. The variety of hot tapas, salads and other snacks draws a well-dressed crowd. No reservations. (☎93 216 03 68; Carrer de Mallorca 236; tapas €3-14; ⏰9am-1.30am; 🚆 FGC Provença)

La Bodegueta Provença — TAPAS €€

21 MAP P112, C3

The 'Little Wine Cellar' offers classic tapas presented with a touch of class, from *calamares a la andaluza* (lightly battered squid rings) to *cecina* (dried cured veal meat). The house speciality is *ous estrellats* (literally 'smashed eggs') – a mix of scrambled egg white, egg yolk, potato and ingredients ranging from foie gras to *morcilla* (black pudding). (☎93 215 17 25; www.provenca.labodegueta.cat; Carrer de Provença 233; tapas €6-15, mains €9.50-16; ⏰7am-1.45am Mon-Fri, 8am-1.45am Sat, 1pm-12.45am Sun; 📶; 🚆 FGC Provença)

Drinking

Monvínic — WINE BAR

22 MAP P112, E4

At this rhapsody to wine, the digital wine list details more than 3000 international varieties searchable by origin, year or grape. Some 50 selections are available by the glass; you can, of course, order by the bottle too. There is an emphasis on affordability, but if you want to splash out, there are fantastic vintage options. (93 272 61 87; www.monvinic.com; Carrer de la Diputació 249; 1-11pm Tue-Fri, 7-11pm Mon & Sat; M Passeig de Gràcia)

Milano
COCKTAIL BAR

23 MAP P112, F5

Completely invisible from street level, this gem of hidden Barcelona nightlife is a subterranean old-school cocktail bar with velvet banquettes and glass-fronted cabinets, presided over by white-jacketed waiters. Live music (Cuban, jazz, blues, flamenco and swing) plays nightly; a DJ takes over after 11pm. Fantastic cocktails include the Picasso (tequila, honey, absinthe and lemon) and six different Bloody Marys. (93 112 71 50; www.campari milano.com; Ronda de la Universitat 35; noon-3am; M Catalunya)

Garage Beer Co
CRAFT BEER

24 MAP P112, C5

One of the first of the slew of craft-beer bars to pop up in Barcelona, Garage brews its own in a space at the bar, and offers around 10 different styles at a time. The eponymous Garage (a delicate session IPA) and Slinger (a more robust IPA) are always present on the board. (93 528 59 89; www.garagebeer.co; Carrer del Consell de Cent 261; 5pm-midnight Mon-Thu, 5pm-2.30am Fri, noon-3am Sat, 2pm-midnight Sun; M Universitat)

Speakeasy

True to its name, **Speakeasy** (Map p112, B3; 93 217 50 80; www.drymartiniorg.com; Carrer d'Aribau 162; mains €18.50-28; 8-11pm Mon-Sat; FGC Provença) is a clandestine restaurant lurking behind the **Dry Martini** bar. You will be shown a door through the open kitchen area to the 'storeroom', lined with hundreds of bottles of backlit, quality tipples. Tempting menu options might include prawn ravioli with parmesan crème or venison with braised celery.

Dry Martini
BAR

25 MAP P112, B3

Waiters make expert cocktail suggestions, but the house drink, taken at the bar or on one of the plush green banquettes, is always a good bet. The gin and tonic comes in an enormous mug-sized glass – one will take you most of the night. (93 217 50 80; www.drymartiniorg.com; Carrer d'Aribau 162-166; 1pm-2.30am Mon-Fri, 6.30pm-2.30am Sat & Sun; FGC Provença)

El Viti
BAR

26 MAP P112, H1

Along the hip Passeig de Sant Joan, El Viti checks all the boxes –

high ceilings, brick walls both bare and glazed, black-clad staff and a barrel of artisanal vermouth on the bar. It also serves a good line in tapas. (93 633 83 36; www.elviti.com; Passeig de Sant Joan 62; noon-midnight Sun-Thu, to 1am Fri & Sat; ; M Tetuan)

Antilla BCN
CLUB

27 MAP P112, B6

The salsateca in town, this is the place to come for Cuban *son*, merengue, salsa and a whole lot more. (93 451 45 64; www.antillasalsa.com; Carrer d'Aragó 141; cover Fri & Sat €10; 10pm-4am Wed, 11pm-4am Thu, 11pm-6am Fri & Sat, 7pm-2am Sun; M Urgell)

City Hall
CLUB

28 MAP P112, F5

A long corridor leads to the dance floor of this venerable and popular club, located in a former theatre. Music styles, from house and other electric sounds to funk, change nightly; check the agenda online. The cover charge includes a drink. (93 238 07 22; www.cityhallbarcelona.com; Rambla de Catalunya 2-4; cover from €10; 10pm-6am Mon, 12.30am-6am Tue-Sun; M Catalunya)

Shopping

Joan Múrria
FOOD & DRINKS

29 MAP P112, E2

Ramon Casas designed the 1898 Modernista shopfront advertisements featured at this culinary temple of speciality food goods from around Catalonia and beyond. Artisan cheeses, Iberian hams, caviar, canned delicacies, smoked fish, *cavas* and wines, coffee and loose-leaf teas are among the treats in store. (93 215 57 89; www.murria.cat; Carrer de Roger de Llúria 85; 10am-8.30pm Tue-Fri, 10am-2pm & 5-8.30pm Sat; M Girona)

Flores Navarro
FLOWERS

30 MAP P112, F2

You never know when you might need flowers, and this florist never closes. Established in 1960, it's a vast space (or couple of spaces, in fact), and worth a visit just for the bank of colour and wonderful fragrance. (93 457 40 99; www.floristeriasnavarro.com; Carrer de València 320; 24hr; M Girona)

Altaïr
BOOKS

31 MAP P112, E5

Enter a wonderland of travel in this extensive bookshop, which has enough guidebooks, maps, travel literature and other books to induce a severe case of itchy feet. It has a travellers noticeboard and, downstairs, a cafe. (93 342 71 71; www.altair.es; Gran Via de les Corts Catalanes 616; 10am-8.30pm Mon-Sat; ; M Catalunya)

El Corte Inglés
DEPARTMENT STORE

32 MAP P112, G5

Spain's only remaining department-store chain stocks everything you'd expect, from computers to cushions and high fashion to homewares. Fabulous city views extend from the top-floor restaurant. Nearby branches include one at **Avinguda Diagonal 471-473** (☎93 493 48 00; Ⓜ Hospital Clínic). (☎93 306 38 00; www.elcorteingles.es; Plaça de Catalunya 23; ⏰9.30am-9pm Mon-Sat; Ⓜ Catalunya)

El Bulevard dels Antiquaris

ANTIQUES

33 🔒 MAP P112, E3

More than 70 stores (be warned most close for lunch) are gathered under one roof to offer the most varied selection of collector's pieces. These range from old porcelain dolls through to fine crystal, from Asian antique furniture to old French goods, and from African and other ethnic art to jewellery.

It's on the floor above the more general **Bulevard Rosa** (☎93 215 83 31; www.bulevardrosa.com; ⏰10.30am-9pm Mon-Sat;) arcade. (☎93 215 44 99; www.bulevarddels antiquaris.com; Passeig de Gràcia 55-57; ⏰10.30am-8.30pm Mon-Sat; Ⓜ Passeig de Gràcia)

Bagués-Masriera

JEWELLERY

34 🔒 MAP P112, E3

This jewellery store, in business since the 19th century, is in thematic harmony with its location in the Modernista Casa Amatller. Some of the classic pieces to come out of the Bagués clan's workshops have an equally playful, Modernista bent. (☎93 216 01 74; www.bagues-masriera.com; Passeig de Gràcia 41; ⏰10am-8.30pm Mon-Fri, 11am-8pm Sat; Ⓜ Passeig de Gràcia)

Products on display at Joan Múrria

Top Sight

La Sagrada Família

Spain's biggest tourist attraction and a work in progress for more than a century, La Sagrada Família is a unique, extraordinary piece of architecture. Conceived as a temple as atonement for Barcelona's sins of modernity, this giant church became Gaudí's holy mission. When completed it will have a capacity for 13,000 and is, in medieval fashion, a work of storytelling art. Rich in iconography and symbolism, at once ancient and thoroughly modern, La Sagrada Família leaves no one unmoved.

93 208 04 14

www.sagradafamilia.org

Carrer de Mallorca 401

adult/child €15/free

9am-8pm Apr-Sep, to 7pm Mar & Oct, to 6pm Nov-Feb

M Sagrada Família

Nativity Facade

This astonishing tapestry in stone is, for now, the single most impressive feature of La Sagrada Família. Step back for an overall sense of this remarkable work, which was the first of the facades completed (in 1930), then draw near to examine the detail. It is replete with sculpted figures (Gaudí used plaster casts of local people as models) and images from nature.

Passion Facade

Symbolically facing the setting sun, the Passion facade – stripped bare and left to speak for itself – is the austere counterpoint to the Nativity facade's riotous decoration. From the Last Supper to his burial, Christ's story plays out in an S-shaped sequence from bottom to top. Check the cryptogram in which the numbers always add up to 33, Jesus' age at crucifixion.

A Hidden Portrait

Careful observation of the Passion Facade will reveal a special tribute from sculptor Josep Subirachs to Gaudí. The central sculptural group (below Christ crucified) shows, from right to left, Christ bearing his cross, Veronica displaying the cloth with Christ's bloody image, a pair of soldiers and, watching it all, a man called the evangelist. Subirachs used a rare photo of Gaudí, taken a couple of years before his death, as the model for the evangelist's face.

Glory Facade

The Glory facade will be the most fanciful of them all, with a narthex boasting 16 hyperboloid lanterns topped by cones that will look something like an organ made of melting ice cream. Gaudí made only general drawings of the facade, but its symbolism is clear: Christ in all his glory and the road to God.

★ Top Tips

- Online tickets give a slight discount, but more importantly allow you to skip what can be very lengthy queues.
- Guided tours (€24) last 50 minutes. Alternatively, take an audio tour (€7), for which you need ID.
- An extra €14 (which includes the audio tour) will get you into lifts that rise inside the towers in the Nativity and Passion facades; this must be prebooked online.
- Hats, see-through clothing, short shorts, low necklines and exposed backs, shoulders and midriffs aren't permitted.

Take a Break

There is nothing of note in the immediate area (it's a hell of tourist pizza joints).

For authentic Mexican fare and a local crowd, seek out **Cantina Mexicana** (93 667 66 68; www.cantinalamexicana.es; Carrer de València 427; mains €7-13; 1pm-midnight; ; M Sagrada Família).

The Interior & Apse

Inside, the roof is held up by a forest of extraordinary angled pillars. As the pillars soar towards the ceiling, they sprout a web of supporting branches, creating the effect of a forest canopy. The tree image is in no way fortuitous – Gaudí envisaged such an effect. Everything was thought through, including the shape and placement of windows to create the mottled effect one would see with sunlight pouring through the branches of a thick forest.

Columns & Stained Glass

The pillars are of four different types of stone. They vary in colour and load-bearing strength, from the soft Montjuïc stone pillars along the lateral aisles through to granite, dark grey basalt and finally burgundy-tinged Iranian porphyry for the key columns at the intersection of the nave and transept. The stained glass, divided in shades of red, blue, green and ochre, creates a hypnotic, magical atmosphere when the sun hits the windows.

Crypt

From the main apse, holes in the floor allow a view down into the crypt, which was the first part of the church to be completed in 1885. Built in a largely neo-Gothic style, it's here that Gaudí lies buried. The crypt has often been used as the main place of worship while the remainder of the church is completed.

Interior of La Sagrada Família

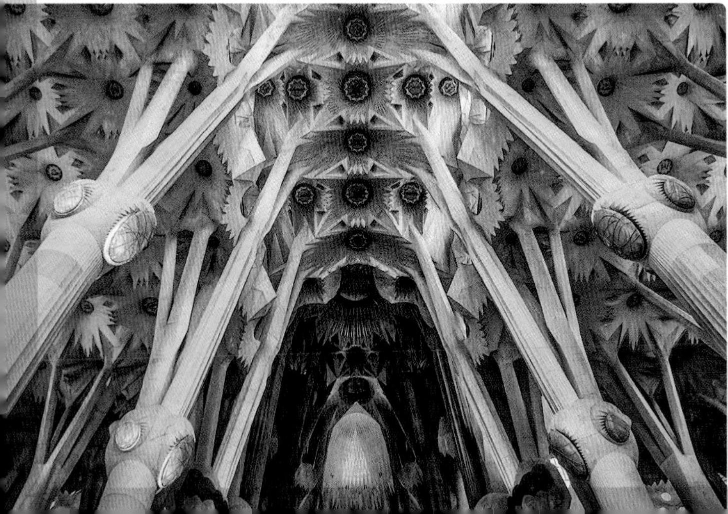

Antoni Gaudí

Antoni Gaudí i Cornet (1852–1926) was born in Reus, trained initially in metalwork and obtained his architecture degree in 1878. Although part of the Modernista movement, Gaudí had a style all his own. A recurring theme was his obsession with the harmony of natural forms. Straight lines are eliminated, and the lines between real and unreal, sober and dreamdrunk are all blurred. The grandeur of his vision was matched by an obsession with detail, as evidenced by his use of lifelike sculpture on the Nativity facade.

With age he became almost exclusively motivated by stark religious conviction and from 1915 he gave up all other projects to devote himself exclusively to La Sagrada Família. When he died in June 1926 (he was knocked down by a tram on Gran Via de les Corts Catalanes) less than a quarter of La Sagrada Família had been completed.

Under construction for over 130 years, the church's estimated completion date is 2026 at the earliest. As Gaudí is reported to have said when questioned about the never-ending project, 'My client is not in a hurry'.

Bell Towers

The towers of the three facades represent the 12 Apostles (so far, eight have been built). Lifts whisk visitors up one tower of the Nativity and Passion facades (the latter gets longer queues) for marvellous views. There will eventually be 18 towers – 12 Apostles, four evangelists, the Virgin Mary and Christ – which when completed will make this the world's tallest church building.

Museu Gaudí

Jammed with old photos, drawings and restored plaster models that bring Gaudí's ambitions to life, the museum also houses an extraordinarily complex plumb-line device he used to calculate his constructions. It's like journeying through the mind of the great architect. Some of the models are upside down, as that's how Gaudí worked to best study the building's form and structural balance.

Explore Gràcia & Park Güell

Gràcia was an independent town until the 1890s, and its narrow lanes and pretty plazas still have a village-like feel. Laid-back cafes and bars, vintage shops and a smattering of multicultural restaurants make it a magnet to a young and partly international crowd. On a hill to the north lies one of Gaudí's most captivating works, the outdoor Modernista storybook of Park Güell.

Park Güell is the standout attraction and can be reached by a long (uphill) walk or metro ride (and shorter walk). Aside from the park, Gràcia doesn't have a dense concentration of sights, but is great for a wander to soak up the village atmosphere.

The liveliest streets and squares are Carrer de Verdi, where you will find wonderful cafes and restaurants, such as Cafè Camèlia (p136); Plaça del Sol, a raucous square ringed with bars; Plaça de la Vila de Gràcia, dotted with cafes and restaurants; family-friendly Plaça de la Revolució de Setembre de 1868, which has a playground, but also benefits from bars such as Bar Canigó (p141). Gràcia is great during the day or at night – the squares are sunny and relaxed for breakfast or lunch, and lively at night with scenesters enjoying a drink al fresco.

Getting There & Around

M Línia 3 (Fontana stop) leaves you halfway up Carrer Gran de Gràcia and close to a network of busy squares. To enter Gràcia from the northern side, take Línia 4 to Joanic.

Neighbourhood Map on p134

Mosaic at Parl Güell (p130) DAVID PEREIRAS/SHUTTERSTOCK ©

Top Sight

Park Güell

Park Güell – north of Gràcia and about 4km from Plaça de Catalunya – is where Gaudí turned his hand to landscape gardening. It's a surreal, enchanting place where the iconic Modernista's passion for natural forms really took flight, to the point where the artificial almost seems more natural than the natural.

MAP P134, B1

www.parkguell.cat

Carrer d'Olot 7

adult/child €8/5.60

8am-9.30pm May-Aug, to 8.30pm Apr, Sep & Oct, to 6.30pm Nov-Mar

24, 92, M Lesseps, Vallcarca

Stairway & Sala Hipóstila

The steps up from the entrance and the two *Hansel and Gretel*–style gatehouses are a mosaic of fountains, ancient Catalan symbols and a much photographed dragon-lizard. Atop the stairs is the Sala Hipóstila, a forest of 86 Doric columns (some of them leaning at an angle and all inspired by ancient Greece); the space was intended as a market.

Banc de Trencadís

Atop the Sala Hipóstila is a broad open space; its highlight is the Banc de Trencadís, a tiled bench curving sinuously around the perimeter and alternately interpreted as a mythical serpent or, typically for Gaudí, waves in the sea. Although Gaudí was responsible for the form, the *trencadís* (broken tile) surface designs were the work of Gaudí's right-hand man, Josep Maria Jujol.

Casa-Museu Gaudí

Above and to the right of the entrance, the spired house you see is the **Casa-Museu Gaudí** (☎93 219 38 11; www.casamuseugaudi.org; Park Güell, Carretera del Carmel 23a; adult/child €5.50/free; ⏲9am-8pm Apr-Sep, 10am-6pm Oct-Mar; 🚌24, 92, 116, Ⓜ Lesseps), where Gaudí lived for almost the last 20 years of his life (1906–26). Furniture he designed (including items that once lived in La Pedrera, Casa Batlló and Casa Calvet) is displayed along with other memorabilia. The house was built in 1904 by Francesc Berenguer i Mestres as a prototype for the 60 or so houses that were originally planned here.

★ Top Tips

- Go first thing in the morning or late in the day to beat the worst of the crowds.
- You can visit the northern part of the park (without the Gaudí features) free of charge.
- The walk from metro stop Lesseps is signposted. From the Vallcarca stop, the walk is marginally shorter and the uphill trek eased by escalators.

✕ Take a Break

Before or after making the trip up to the park, stop off at **La Panxa del Bisbe** (☎93 213 70 49; Carrer del Torrent de les Flors 158; tapas €8.50-15, tasting menus €28-36; ⏲1.30-3.30pm & 8.30pm-midnight Tue-Sat; Ⓜ Joanic) for deliciously creative tapas and good wines.

The park makes a spectacular setting for a picnic; bring supplies with you as there's nowhere to stock up nearby.

Walking Tour

Village Life in Gràcia

Located halfway between L'Eixample and Park Güell, Gràcia was a separate village until 1897, and its tight, narrow lanes and endless interlocking squares maintain a unique, almost village-like identity to this day. In places bohemian, in others rapidly gentrifying, Gràcia is Barcelona at its most eclectic, its nooks and crannies home to everything from amber lit old taverns to eco-minded boutiques.

Walk Facts

Start Bar Bodega Quimet

End La Cigale

Length 2km; all day

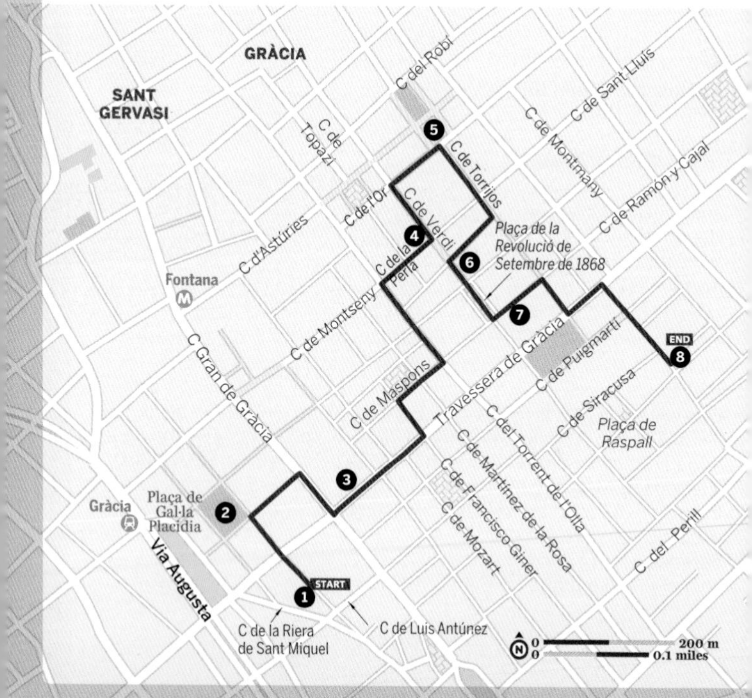

❶ Catalan Classic

A remnant from a bygone age, **Bar Bodega Quimet** (p137) is a delightfully atmospheric spot, with old bottles lining the walls, a burnished wooden bar and a seemingly exhaustive list of tapas.

❷ Local Market

Built in the 1870s and covered in fizzy Modernista style in 1893, the **Mercat de la Llibertat** (p136) was designed by Francesc Berenguer i Mestres, Gaudí's long-time assistant.

❸ Cruelty-Free Style

At **Amapola Vegan Shop** (p142), stylish clothing and accessories are all made from animal-free materials. You'll find sleek messenger bags, ballerina-style flats and cheeky T-shirts with slogans like 'Another Fucking Vegan' and 'No como mis amigos' (I don't eat my friends).

❹ Fashion and Homeware

Picnic (☎93 016 69 53; www.picnicstore.es; Carrer de Verdi 17; ⏰11am-9pm Mon-Fri, 11am-3pm & 4-9pm Sat; Ⓜ Fontana) is a tiny, beautifully curated boutique with stylish sneakers by Meyba, striped jerseys from Basque label Loreak Meridian and boldly patterned Mödernaked backpacks. Other finds include animal-print ceramics for the home, small-scale art prints and fashion mags.

❺ Plaça de la Virreina

Thanks to the low-slung houses along one side and the 17th-century Església de Sant Joan on the other, Plaça de la Virreina is one of the most village-like of Gràcia's squares. With its outdoor tables, it's a lively hub for locals.

❻ Local Bar

Bar Canigò (p141) is a corner bar on an animated square and a timeless locals' spot to sip a beer and chat. It's especially welcoming in winter.

❼ Cafe Culture

La Nena (p137) is a neighbourhood favourite for its *suïssos* (hot chocolate) and *melindros* (spongy sweet biscuits). The area out the back is designed to keep kids busy, with toys, books and a blackboard.

❽ Cocktail Den

La Cigale (☎93 457 58 23; www.facebook.com/la-cigale-barcelona; Carrer de Tordera 50; ⏰6pm-2am Sun-Thu, to 3am Fri & Sat; Ⓜ Joanic) is a civilised place for a drink, with oil paintings on the walls, gilded mirrors and leatherbound volumes scattered about. Music is chilled, conversation lively, and you're likely to see Charlie Chaplin in action on the silent flat-screen TV.

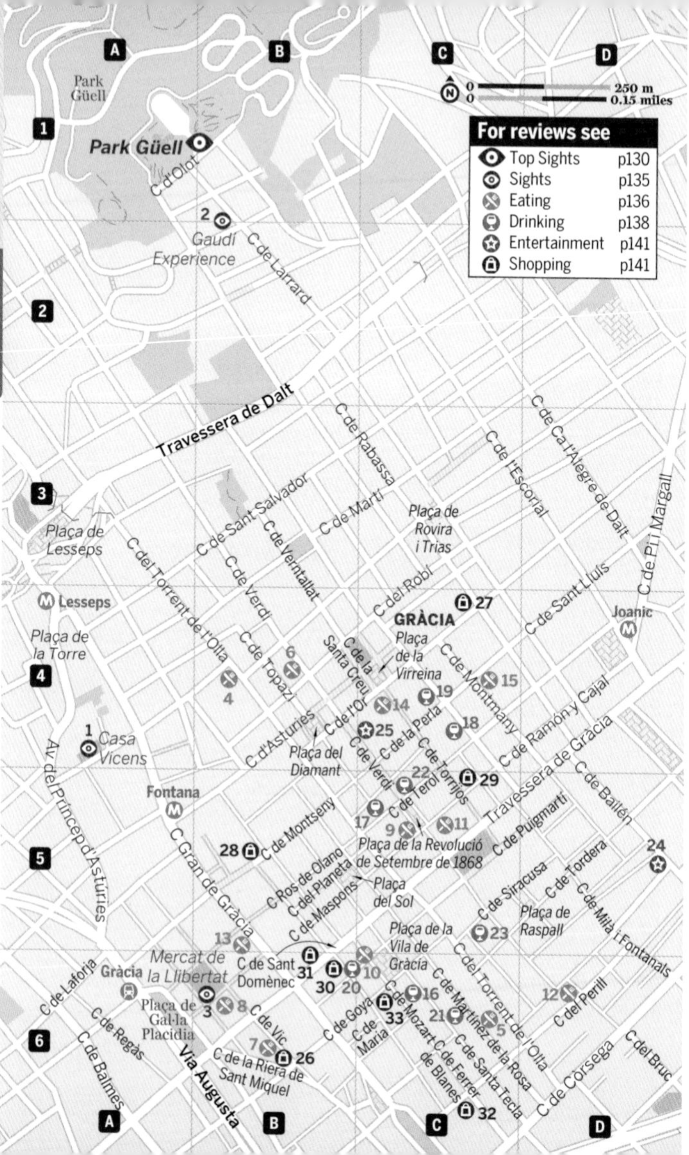
For reviews see
Top Sights p130
Sights p135
Eating p136
Drinking p138
Entertainment p141
Shopping p141
0 250 m
0 0.15 miles
Park Güell
Park Güell
C d'Olot
Gaudí Experience
C de Larrard
Travessera de Dalt
C de Rabassa
C de l'Escorial
C de Ca l'Alegre de Dalt
C de Pi i Margall
C de Sant Salvador
C de Martí
Plaça de Rovira i Trias
C de Verntallat
C de Verdi
C del Torrent de l'Olla
Plaça de Lesseps
Lesseps
Plaça de la Torre
C del Robí
GRÀCIA
Plaça de la Virreina
C de Sant Lluís
Joanic
C de la Santa Creu
C de Topazi
C de Montmany
C de Ramón y Cajal
C d'Asturies
C de l'Or
C de la Perla
Plaça del Diamant
C de Verdi
C de Torrijos
Travessera de Gràcia
C de Bailèn
Casa Vicens
Av del Príncep d'Astúries
Fontana
C de Terol
C de Puigmartí
C de Montseny
Plaça de la Revolució de Setembre de 1868
C Gran de Gràcia
C Ros de Olano
C del Planeta
C de Maspons
Plaça del Sol
C de Siracusa
C de Tordera
Plaça de Raspall
C de Milà i Fontanals
Plaça de la Vila de Gràcia
Mercat de la Llibertat
C de Sant Domènec
C de Laforja
Gràcia
Plaça de Gal·la Placidia
C de Vic
C de Goya
C de Maria
C de Mozart
C de Martínez de la Rosa
C del Torrent de l'Olla
C del Perill
C de Regàs
C de Balmes
Via Augusta
C de la Riera de Sant Miquel
C de Ferrer de Blanes
C de Santa Tecla
C de Còrsega
C del Bruc

Sights

Casa Vicens

MUSEUM

1 MAP P134, A4

A Unesco-listed masterpiece, Casa Vicens was first opened regularly to the public in 2017. The angular, turreted 1885-completed private house created for stock and currency broker Manuel Vicens i Montaner was Gaudí's inaugural commission, when the architect was aged just 30. Tucked away west of Gràcia's main drag, the richly detailed facade is awash with ceramic colour and shape. You're free to wander through at your own pace but 30-minute guided tours (available in English) bring the building to life. (93 348 42 58; www.casavicens.org; Carrer de les Carolines 18-24; adult/child €16/14, guided tour per person additional €3; 10am-8pm, last tour 7.30pm; M Fontana)

Gaudí Experience

MUSEUM

2 MAP P134, B1

The Gaudí Experience is a fun-filled Disney-style look at the life and work of Barcelona's favourite son, just a stone's throw from Park Güell. There are models of his buildings and whizz-bang interactive exhibits and touchscreens, but the highlight is the stomach-churning 4D presentation in its tiny screening room. Not recommended for the frail or children aged under six years. (93 285 44 40; www.gaudiexperiencia.com; Carrer de Larrard 41; adult/child €9/7.50; 10.30am-7pm Apr-Sep, to 5pm Oct-Mar; M Lesseps)

Facade of Casa Vicens

Vila de Gràcia

Gràcia's busiest square, the Plaça de la Vila de Gràcia, was, until a few years ago, known as Plaça de Rius i Taulet, and you'll still hear that name mentioned occasionally. Some locals refer to it as the Plaça del Rellotge ('Clock') for the tall clock tower that stands here.

Mercat de la Llibertat MUSEUM

3 MAP P134, B6

Opened in 1888, the 'Market of Liberty' was covered over in 1893 by Francesc Berenguer i Mestres (1866–1914), Gaudí's long-time assistant, in typically fizzy Modernista style, employing generous whirls of wrought iron. It received a considerable facelift in 2009 but remains emblematic of the Gràcia district: full of life and fabulous fresh produce. (93 217 09 95; www.mercatsbcn.com; Plaça de la Llibertat 27; 8am-8pm Mon-Fri, to 3pm Sat; FGC Gràcia)

Eating

Chivuo's BURGERS €

4 MAP P134, B4

Burgers and craft beers make a fine pair at this buzzing den. A mostly local crowd comes for huge burgers (served rare unless you specify otherwise) with house-made sauces – best ordered with fluffy, golden-fried *fritas* (chips). Mostly Catalan and Spanish brews, including excellent offerings from Barcelona-based Edge Brewing, Catalan Brewery, Napar and Garage Beer, rotate on the eight taps. (93 218 51 34; www.chivuos.com; Carrer del Torrent de l'Olla 175; burgers €7-9; 1-5pm & 7pm-midnight Mon-Sat; M Fontana)

Con Gracia FUSION €€€

5 MAP P134, C6

This teeny hideaway (seating about 20 in total) is a hive of originality, producing delicately balanced Mediterranean cuisine with Asian touches. On offer is a regularly changing surprise tasting menu or the set 'traditional' one (both six courses), with dishes such as squid stuffed with *jamón ibérico* and black truffle, and sake-marinated tuna with walnut pesto. Book ahead. (93 238 02 01; www.congracia.es; Carrer de Martínez de la Rosa 8; tasting menus €65, with wine €95; 7-11pm Tue-Sat; M Diagonal)

Cafè Camèlia VEGETARIAN €

6 MAP P134, B4

A peaceful spot for coffee, set lunches and desserts, this pretty little vegetarian cafe has a small menu of well-executed dishes – hummus, vegetable curry, open-faced sandwiches, quinoa burgers with roasted vegetables and a risotto of the day. (93 415 36 86; Carrer de Verdi 79; mains €7.50-11.50;

10am-midnight Mon-Sat, to 9pm Sun; ; Fontana)

Bar Bodega Quimet

TAPAS €

7 MAP P134, B6

A remnant from a bygone age, Bar Bodega Quimet is a delightfully atmospheric bar, with old bottles lining the walls, marble tables and a burnished wooden bar. The list of tapas and seafood is almost exhaustive, while another house speciality is *torrades* – huge slabs of toasted white bread topped with cured meats, fresh anchovies and sardines. (93 218 41 89; Carrer de Vic 23; tapas €3-11.50; 10am-11.30pm Mon-Fri, noon-11.30pm Sat & Sun; Fontana)

La Pubilla

CATALAN €

8 MAP P134, B6

Hidden away by the Mercat de la Llibertat, La Pubilla specialises in hearty *'esmorzars de forquilla'* ('fork breakfasts') beloved by market workers and nearby residents. There's also a daily three-course *menú del día* for €16, which includes Catalan dishes such as baked cod, or roast pork cheek with chickpeas. Arrive early for a chance of a table. (93 218 29 94; Plaça de la Llibertat 23; mains €8-13.50; 8.30am-5pm Mon, to midnight Tue-Sat; Fontana)

Pepa Tomate

TAPAS €€

9 MAP P134, C5

This casual tapas spot on Plaça de la Revolució de Setembre de 1868 is popular at all hours of the day. Fresh produce takes front and centre on the wide-ranging menu in dishes like fried green tomatoes, Andalucian baby squid, tandoori lamb tacos, Iberian pork or mushroom, croquettes, and carrot gazpacho in summer. (93 210 46 98; www.pepatomategrup.com; Plaça de la Revolució de Setembre de 1868 17; sharing plates €7-17; 8pm-midnight Mon, from 9am Tue-Fri, from 10am Sat, from 11am Sun; ; Fontana)

Café Godot

INTERNATIONAL €€

10 MAP P134, C6

A stylish space of exposed brick, timber and tiles, opening to a garden out back, Godot is a relaxing place with an extensive menu, ranging from white-wine-steamed mussels and scallops with Thai-style green curry to duck confit with lentils and spinach. Brunch is an American-style affair with eggs, crispy bacon and fluffy pancakes. (93 368 20 36; www.cafegodot.com; Carrer de Sant Domènec 19; mains €10-18.50; 10am-1am Mon-Fri, 11am-2am Sat & Sun; Fontana)

La Nena

CAFE €

11 MAP P134, C5

At this delightfully chaotic space, indulge in cups of *suïssos* (rich hot chocolate) served with a plate of heavy homemade whipped cream and *melindros* (spongy sweet biscuits), desserts and a few savoury dishes (including crêpes). The place is strewn with books, and you can play with the board games on the shelves. (93 285 14 76; www.facebook.com/chocolaterialanena; Carrer de Ramon i Cajal 36; dishes €2-4.50; 8.30am-10.30pm Mon-Fri, 9am-10.30pm Sat & Sun; ; M Fontana)

Bilbao

SPANISH €€

12 MAP P134, D6

Behind its unassuming exterior, Bilbao is a timeless classic, where reservations for dinner are imperative. The back dining room, with bottle-lined walls, stout timber tables and sepia lighting evocative of a country tavern, sets the stage for feasting on hearty dishes like oxtail in red wine sauce, grilled pork trotters and codfish with garlic mousse, accompanied by good Spanish wines. (93 458 96 24; www.restaurantbilbao.com; Carrer del Perill 33; mains €16-30; 1-4pm & 9-11pm Mon-Fri, 2-4pm & 9-11pm Sat, closed Aug; M Diagonal)

Botafumeiro

SEAFOOD €€€

13 MAP P134, B5

This temple of Galician shellfish has long been a magnet for VIPs visiting Barcelona. You can bring the price down by sharing a few *medias raciones* (large tapas plates) to taste a range of marine offerings followed by mains like spider crab pie, squid ink paella or grilled spiny lobster. (93 218 42 30; www.botafumeiro.es; Carrer Gran de Gràcia 81; mains €22-59; noon-1am; M Fontana)

Cantina Machito

MEXICAN €€

14 MAP P134, C4

On a leafy street, colourful Machito – adorned with Frida Kahlo images – gets busy with locals, and the outside tables are a great place to eat and drink until late. Start with a *michelada* (spicy beer cocktail) before dining on Mexican delights like quesadillas, tacos and enchiladas. Refreshing iced waters are flavoured with honey and lime or mint and fruit. (93 217 34 14; Carrer de Torrijos 47; mains €9.50-16.50; 1-4pm & 7pm-1am; M Fontana, Joanic)

El Glop

CATALAN €€

15 MAP P134, C4

This raucous restaurant is decked out in country Catalan fashion, with gingham tablecloths and no-nonsense, slap-up meals. The secret is hearty portions of simple dishes, such as *cordero a la brasa* (grilled lamb), *paella de pescado y marisco* (fish and seafood paella) and appetisers like *berenjenas rellenas* (stuffed aubergines) or *calçots* (spring onions) in winter. (93 213 70 58; www.elglop.com; Carrer de Sant Lluís 24; mains €8-20; 1pm-midnight Mon-Fri, noon-midnight Sat & Sun; M Joanic)

Drinking

Bobby Gin

COCKTAIL BAR

16 MAP P134, C6

With over 60 varieties, this whitewashed stone-walled bar

is a haven for gin lovers. Try an infusion-based concoction (rose-tea-infused Hendrick's with strawberries and lime; tangerine-infused Tanqueray 10 with agave nectar and bitter chamomile) or a cocktail like the Santa Maria (chardonnay, milk-thistle syrup, thyme, sage and lemon). Fusion tapas choices include G&T-cured salmon. (☎93 368 18 92; www.bobbygin.com; Carrer de Francisco Giner 47; ⏰4pm-2am Sun-Wed, to 2.30am Thu, to 3am Fri & Sat; M Diagonal)

Viblioteca

WINE BAR

17 MAP P134, C5

A glass cabinet piled high with ripe cheese (over 50 varieties) entices you into this small, white, cleverly designed contemporary space. The real speciality at Viblioteca, however, is wine, and you can choose from 150 mostly local labels, many of them available by the glass. (☎93 284 42 02; www.viblioteca.com; Carrer de Vallfogona 12; ⏰7pm-midnight; M Fontana)

Rabipelao

COCKTAIL BAR

18 MAP P134, C4

An anchor of Gràcia's nightlife, Rabipelao is a celebratory space with a shiny disco ball and DJs spinning salsa beats. A silent film plays in one corner beyond the red velvety wallpaper-covered walls and there's a richly hued mural above the bar. Tropical cocktails like mojitos and caipirinhas pair with South American snacks such as *arepas* (meat-filled cornbread patties) and

Plaça de la Vila de Gràcia (p136)

Worth a Trip: The Carmel Bunkers

For a magnificent view over the city that's well off the beaten path, head to the neighbourhood of El Carmel and make the ascent up the hill known as **Turó de la Rovira** (Bunkers del Carmel; 93 256 21 22; www.museuhistoria.bcn.cat; Carrer de Marià Labèrnia; admission free; museum 10am-2pm Wed, 10am-3pm Sat & Sun; V17, 119) to the Bunkers del Carmel viewpoint. Above the weeds and dusty hillside, you'll find the old concrete platforms that were once part of anti-aircraft battery during the Spanish Civil War (in the postwar, it was a shanty town until the early 1990s, and has lain abandoned since then). There is a small information centre/museum.

To get to the park, when you arrive at the neighbourhood of El Carmel, have the bus driver tell you when you're near the bunkers. From the bus stop, it's a further 10-minute walk to the viewpoint.

ceviche. (93 182 50 35; www.elrabipelao.com; Carrer del Torrent d'En Vidalet 22; 7pm-1.30am Sun-Thu, to 3am Fri & Sat, 1-4.30pm Sun; M Joanic)

Elephanta

BAR

19 MAP P134, C4

Tucked off the main drag, this petite cocktail bar has an old-fashioned vibe, with long plush green banquettes, art-lined walls and a five-seat bar with vintage wood stools. Gin is the drink of choice, with more than 40 varieties on hand, and the cocktails are expertly mixed. (93 237 69 06; www.elephanta.cat; Carrer del Torrent d'en Vidalet 37; 6pm-1.30am Mon-Wed, to 2.30am Thu, to 3am Fri & Sat, to 10pm Sun; ; M Joanic)

La Vermu

BAR

20 MAP P134, B6

House-made *negre* (black) and *blanc* (white) vermouth, served with a slice of orange and an olive, is the speciality of this hip neighbourhood hang-out. The airy space with exposed timber beams and industrial lighting centres on a marble bar with seating and surrounding marble-topped tables. Vermouth aside, it also has a small but stellar wine list and stylishly presented tapas. (93 171 80 87; Carrer de Sant Domènec 15; 6.30pm-midnight Mon-Thu, 12.30-4.30pm & 7.30pm-12.30am Fri-Sun; FGC Gràcia)

El Sabor

BAR

21 MAP P134, C6

Ruled since 1992 by the charismatic Havana-born Angelito is this home of *ron y son* (rum and sound). A mixed crowd of Cubans and fans of the Caribbean island come to drink mojitos and shake their stuff in this diminutive, good-humoured hang-out. Stop by on Mondays, Tuesdays and Wednesdays for a free two-hour salsa or bachata lesson (starting at 9.30pm). (☎674 993075; Carrer de Francisco Giner 32; ⏲9pm-2.30am Sun-Thu, to 3am Fri & Sat; M Diagonal)

Bar Canigó BAR

22 MAP P134, C5

Now run by the third generation of owners, this corner bar overlooking Plaça de la Revolució de Setembre de 1868 is an animated spot to sip on a house vermouth or an Estrella beer around rickety old marble-top tables, as people have done here since 1922. (☎93 213 30 49; www.barcanigo.com; Carrer de Verdi 2; ⏲10am-2am Mon-Thu, 10am-3am Fri, 8pm-3am Sat; M Fontana)

Raïm BAR

23 MAP P134, C5

The walls in Raïm are alive with black-and-white photos of Cubans and Cuba. Weathered old wooden chairs of another epoch huddle around marble tables, while grand old wood-framed mirrors hang from the walls. It draws a friendly, garrulous crowd who pile in for first-rate mojitos and an excellent selection of rum. (Carrer del Progrés 48; ⏲8pm-2am Tue-Thu, to 3am Fri & Sat; M Diagonal)

Entertainment

Cine Texas CINEMA

24 MAP P134, D5

All films at this contemporary four-screen cinema are shown in their original languages (with subtitles in Catalan). Genres span art house through to Hollywood blockbusters. Catalan-language films are subtitled in English. (☎93 348 77 48; www.cinemestexas.cat; Carrer de Bailèn 205; M Joanic)

Verdi CINEMA

25 MAP P134, C4

In the heart of Gràcia, this five-screen cinema shows art-house and blockbuster films in their original language as well as films in Catalan and Spanish. It's handy to lots of local eateries and bars for pre- and post-film enjoyment. (☎93 238 79 90; www.cines-verdi.com; Carrer de Verdi 32; M Fontana)

Shopping

Colmillo de Morsa FASHION & ACCESSORIES

26 MAP P134, B6

Design team Javier Blanco and Elisabet Vallecillo have made waves at Madrid's Cibeles Fashion Week and Paris' fashion fair Who's Next, and showcase their Barcelona-made women's fashion here at their flagship boutique. They've also opened the floor to promote other young, up-and-coming local labels. The light-filled space also hosts art, graphic design and photography exhibitions and fashion shows. (645 206365; www.facebook.com/colmillodemorsa; Carrer de Vic 15-17; 4.30-8.30pm Mon, 11am-2.30pm & 4.30-8.30pm Tue-Sat; FGC Gràcia)

Family Beer

DRINKS

27 MAP P134, C4

Over 130 varieties of local and international craft beers and ciders are stocked in the fridges here, so you can pick up a cold brew to go. It also has brewing kits and books, and runs regular brewing workshops (three hours €45) and hosts free demonstrations of cheese making and cookery using beer, as well as 'meet the brewer' tastings. (93 219 29 88; www.family-beer.com; Carrer de Joan Blanques 55; 5-8.30pm Mon, 10am-2pm & 5-8.30pm Tue-Sat; M Joanic)

Hibernian

BOOKS

28 MAP P134, B5

Barcelona's biggest secondhand English bookshop stocks thousands of titles covering all sorts of subjects, from cookery to children's classics. There's a smaller collection of new books in English too. (93 217 47 96; www.hibernian-books.com; Carrer de Montseny 17; 4-8.30pm Mon, 11am-8.30pm Tue-Sat; M Fontana)

Vinil Vintage

MUSIC

29 MAP P134, C5

Crate diggers will love rummaging through the vinyl collection here. There's a huge range of rock, pop and jazz, including plenty of Spanish music. It also sells turntables and speakers. (93 192 39 99; Carrer de Ramón y Cajal 45-47; 10.30am-2pm & 5-8.30pm Tue-Sat; M Joanic)

Lady Loquita

CLOTHING

30 MAP P134, B6

At this hip little shop you can browse through light, locally made summer dresses by Tiralahilacha, evening wear by Japamala and handmade jewellery by local design label Klimbim. There are also whimsical odds and ends: dinner plates with dog-people portraits and digital prints on wood by About Paola. (93 217 82 92; www.ladyloquita.com; Travessera de Gràcia 126; 11am-2pm & 5-8.30pm Mon-Sat; M Fontana)

Amapola Vegan Shop

CLOTHING

31 MAP P134, B6

A shop with a heart of gold, Amapola proves that you need not toss your ethics aside in the quest for stylish clothing and accessories. You'll find sleek leather-alternatives for wallets, handbags and messenger bags by Matt & Nat, belts by Nae Vic, and elegant scarves by Barts. (93 010 62 73;

Viblioteca (p139)

www.amapolaveganshop.com; Travessera de Gràcia 129; ⏲11am-2pm & 5-8.30pm Mon-Sat; MFontana)

Bodega Bonavista

WINE

32 MAP P134, C6

An excellent little neighbourhood bodega, Bonavista endeavours to seek out great wines at reasonable prices. The stock is mostly from Catalonia and elsewhere in Spain, but there's also a well-chosen selection from France. The Bonavista also acts as a deli, and there are some especially good cheeses. You can sample wines by the glass, along with cheeses and charcuterie, at one of the in-store tables. (☎93 218 81 99; Carrer de Bonavista 10; ⏲10am-2.30pm & 5-9pm Mon-Fri, noon-3pm & 6-9pm Sat, noon-3pm Sun; MFontana)

Nostàlgic

PHOTOGRAPHY

33 MAP P134, C6

In a beautiful space with exposed brick walls and wooden furniture, Nostàlgic specialises in all kinds of modern and vintage photography equipment. You'll find camera bags and tripods for the digital snappers, rolls of film, and quirky Lomo cameras. There is also a decent collection of photography books to buy or browse. (☎93 368 57 57; www.nostalgic.es; Carrer de Goya 18; ⏲10.30am-2pm & 5-8pm Mon-Fri, 11am-2.30pm Sat; MFontana)

Explore

Camp Nou, Pedralbes & Sarrià

Some of Barcelona's most sacred sights are situated within the huge expanse stretching northwest beyond L'Eixample. One is the peaceful medieval monastery of Pedralbes; another is the great shrine to Catalan football, Camp Nou. Other reasons to venture here include an amusement park and great views atop Tibidabo, the wooded trails of Parc de Collserola, and a whizz-bang, kid-friendly science museum.

The massive stadium of Camp Nou (p146; 'New Field' in Catalan) is home to the legendary Futbol Club Barcelona. Attending a game amid the roar of the crowds is an unforgettable experience; the season runs from September to May. Alternatively, get a taste of all the excitement at the interactive Camp Nou Experience (p146), which includes a tour of the stadium. Afterwards, head up to Vivanda (p151) for an outstanding lunch.

After lunch, walk it off along the narrow lanes of old Sarrià. Stop in for a snack of the famed patatas bravas at Bar Tomàs (p150). Stroll over (or take a taxi) to the atmospheric Museu-Monestir de Pedralbes (p149), where you can spend the rest of the afternoon exploring this well-preserved medieval monastery.

The best way to end the night is at an FC Barcelona game at Camp Nou, followed perhaps by celebratory drinks at Lizarran (p147). Afterwards, head over to lovely Plaça de la Concòrdia for a nightcap at El Maravillas (p152).

Getting There & Around

M Línia 3 is handy for the Jardins del Laberint d'Horta (Mundet), and Camp Nou and Palau Reial de Pedralbes (Palau Reial).

Neighbourhood Map on p148

Facade of Bellesguard (p150) ALBUM/ALAMY STOCK PHOTO ©

Top Sight

Camp Nou & the Museu del FC Barcelona

While nothing compares to the excitement of attending a live match, the Camp Nou Experience is a must for football fans. On this self-guided visit of FC Barcelona's home ground, you'll get an in-depth look at the club, starting with a museum filled with multimedia exhibits, trophies and historical displays, followed by a tour of the stadium.

MAP P148, A5

902 189900

www.fcbarcelona.com

Gate 9, Avinguda de Joan XXIII

adult/child €25/20

9.30am-7.30pm Apr-Sep, 10am-6.30pm Mon-Sat, to 2.30pm Sun Oct-Mar

M Palau Reial

A Real, Live Game

Tours of an empty stadium are one thing, but there's nothing like turning up to watch Barça strut their stuff live. Buying tickets is possible online, at FC Botiga shops and at tourist offices. You can also purchase at the Camp Nou ticket office (Gate 9).

Camp Nou Experience

On this self-guided tour, you'll get an in-depth look at the club, starting with a museum filled with multimedia exhibits, trophies and historical displays, followed by a tour of the stadium. It begins in FC Barcelona's museum, which has goal videos, trophies and displays on the club's history, its social commitment and connection to Catalan identity.

Behind The Scenes

The Camp Nou Experience tour takes in the visiting team's dressing room, heads out through the tunnel, and on to the edge of the pitch: standing where so many football greats once stood can be a powerful experience for FCB fans. You'll also get to visit the television studio, the press room and the commentary boxes. Set aside about 2½ hours for the whole visit.

FC Barcelona Megastore

Whether you're heading to a game or visiting the Camp Nou Experience, don't miss the sprawling three-storey **FC Botiga Megastore** (☎93 409 02 71; www.fcbmegastore.com; Gate 9, off Avinguda Joan de XXIII; ⏰10am-7pm Mon-Sat, 10.30am-3.30pm Sun, until kick-off match days; Ⓜ Palau Reial) on the grounds of the stadium. You'll find all manner of goods emblazoned with Barça's famous scarlet and blue insignia. Via touchscreens, you can even order a customised shirt with your name and preferred number that will be ready for you that same day.

★ Top Tips

- Plan your self-guided visit for early in the day to avoid the worst of the crowds – particularly during the warmer months.
- You can purchase Camp Nou Experience tickets from vending machines at Gate 9. No need to wait in line.
- Camp Nou's FC Botiga Megastore has three floors of Barça merchandise.

Take a Break

Just inside the gates (but outside the stadium itself), you'll find a handful of open-air eating and drinking spots, including a branch of star chef Carles Abellán's Tapas 24, an excellent place for drinks and snacks.

You can also grab tapas and drinks at **Lizarran** (www.lizarran.es; Carrer de Can Bruixa 6; ⏰8am-midnight Sun-Thu, to 2am Fri & Sat; Ⓜ Les Corts), located 1km northeast of Camp Nou off Travessera de les Corts.

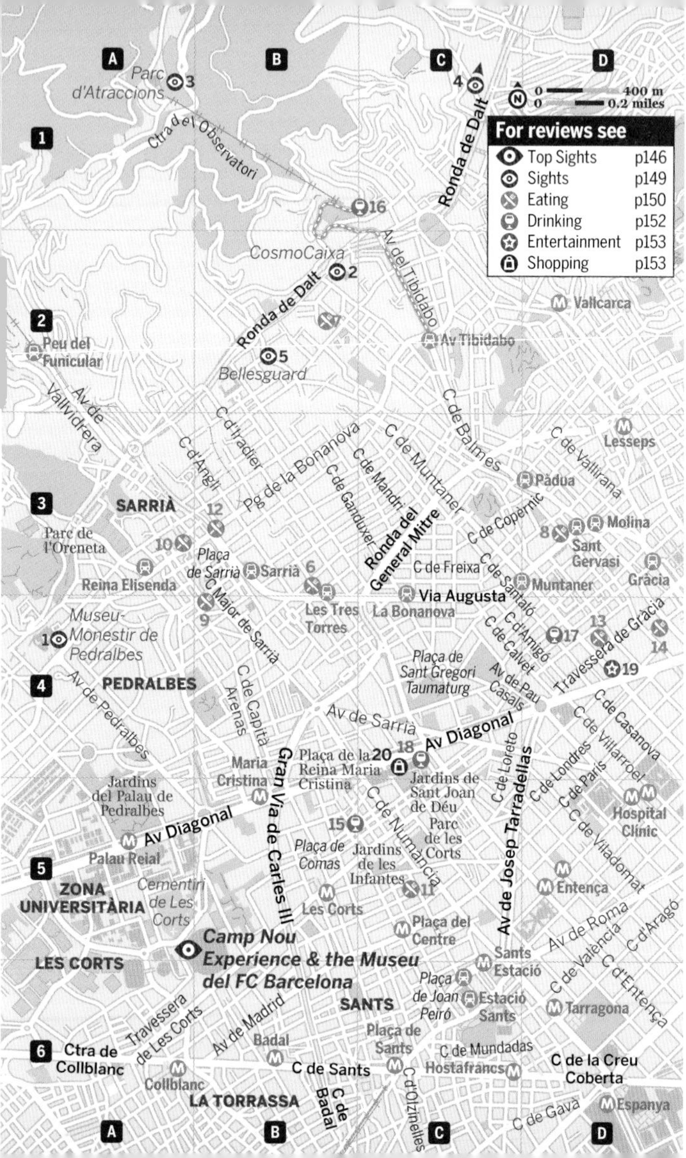
A
B
C
D
1
2
3
4
5
6
0 400 m
0 0.2 miles
For reviews see
Top Sights p146
Sights p149
Eating p150
Drinking p152
Entertainment p153
Shopping p153
Parc d'Atraccions
Ctra de l'Observatori
Ronda de Dalt
CosmoCaixa
Av del Tibidabo
Vallcarca
Av Tibidabo
Peu del Funicular
Bellesguard
Av de Vallvidrera
C d'Iradier
C d'Anglí
Pg de la Bonanova
C de Ganduxer
C de Mandri
C de Muntaner
C de Balmes
C de Vallirana
Lesseps
Pàdua
SARRIÀ
Parc de l'Oreneta
Plaça de Sarrià
Sarrià
Reina Elisenda
Ronda del General Mitre
C de Copèrnic
Molina
Sant Gervasi
Gràcia
C de Freixa
C de Santaló
Muntaner
Via Augusta
Les Tres Torres
La Bonanova
C Major de Sarrià
Museu-Monestir de Pedralbes
C d'Amigó
C de Calvet
Travessera de Gràcia
Plaça de Sant Gregori Taumaturg
Av de Pau Casals
PEDRALBES
Av de Pedralbes
C de Capità Arenas
Av de Sarrià
Av Diagonal
C de Casanova
C de Villarroel
C de Londres
C de París
Plaça de la Reina Maria Cristina
Maria Cristina
Gran Via de Carles III
Jardins de Sant Joan de Déu
C de Loreto
Av de Josep Tarradellas
Jardins del Palau de Pedralbes
C de Numància
Hospital Clínic
Palau Reial
Plaça de Comas
Jardins de les Infantes
Parc de les Corts
C de Viladomat
ZONA UNIVERSITÀRIA
Cementiri de Les Corts
Les Corts
Entença
Plaça del Centre
Av de Roma
C d'Aragó
Camp Nou Experience & the Museu del FC Barcelona
LES CORTS
Sants Estació
Plaça de Joan Peiró
Estació Sants
C de València
C d'Entença
SANTS
Tarragona
Travessera de Les Corts
Av de Madrid
Ctra de Collblanc
Badal
Plaça de Sants
C de Mundadas
C de Sants
Hostafrancs
C de la Creu Coberta
Collblanc
C de Badal
C d'Olzinelles
LA TORRASSA
C de Gavà
Espanya

Sights

Museu-Monestir de Pedralbes MONASTERY

1 MAP P148, A4

Founded in 1326, this serene convent was first opened to the public in 1983 and is now a museum of monastic life (the few remaining nuns have moved into more modern neighbouring buildings). It stands at the top of Avinguda de Pedralbes in a residential area that was countryside until the 20th century, and which remains a divinely quiet corner of Barcelona. (93 256 34 34; http://monestirpedralbes.bcn.cat; Baixada del Monestir 9; adult/child €5/free, after 3pm Sun free; 10am-5pm Tue-Fri, to 7pm Sat, to 8pm Sun Apr-Sep, 10am-2pm Tue-Fri, to 5pm Sat & Sun Oct-Mar; 63, 68, 75, 78, H4, FGC Reina Elisenda)

CosmoCaixa MUSEUM

2 MAP P148, B2

Kids (and kids at heart) are fascinated by displays at this science museum. The single greatest highlight is the re-creation of over 1 sq km of flooded **Amazon** rainforest (Bosc Inundat). More than 100 species of Amazon flora and fauna (including anacondas, colourful poisonous frogs, and caimans) prosper in this unique, living diorama in which you can even experience a tropical downpour. (Museu de la Ciència; 93 212 60 50; www.cosmocaixa.com; Carrer d'Isaac Newton 26; adult/child €4/free, guided tours from €2, planetarium €4; 10am-8pm Tue-Sun; 60, 196)

Parc d'Atraccions AMUSEMENT PARK

3 MAP P148, A1

The reason most *barcelonins* come up to Tibidabo is for some thrills at this funfair, close to the top funicular station. Here you'll find whirling high-speed rides and high-tech 4D cinema, as well as old-fashioned amusements including an old steam train and the Museu d'Autòmats, with automated puppets dating as far back as 1880. Check the website for seasonal opening times. (93 211 79 42; www.tibidabo.cat; Plaça de Tibidabo 3-4; adult/child €28.50/10.30; closed Jan & Feb; T2A, Funicular del Tibidabo)

Jardins del Laberint d'Horta GARDENS

4 MAP P148, C1

Laid out in the late 18th century by Antoni Desvalls, Marquès d'Alfarràs i de Llupià, this carefully manicured park remained a private family idyll until the 1970s, when it was opened to the public. The *laberint* ('labyrinth' in Catalan) refers to the central maze; other paths take you past a pleasant artificial lake, waterfalls, a neoclassical pavilion and a false cemetery. The last is inspired by 19th-century romanticism, characterised by an obsession with a swooning vision of death. (93 413 24 00; http://lameva.barcelona.cat; Passeig del Castanyers 1; adult/child €2.23/1.42, free Wed & Sun; 10am-8pm Apr-Oct, to 7pm Dec-Mar; M Mundet)

Bellesguard

ARCHITECTURE

5 MAP P148, B2

This Gaudí masterpiece was rescued from obscurity and opened to the public in 2013. Built between 1900 and 1909, this private residence (still owned by the original Guilera family) has a castle-like appearance with crenellated walls of stone and brick, narrow stained-glass windows, elaborate ironwork and a soaring turret mounted by a Gaudían cross. It's a fascinating work that combines both Gothic and Modernista elements. (93 250 40 93; www.bellesguardgaudi.com; Carrer de Bellesguard 16; adult/child €9/free; 10am-3pm Tue-Sun; FGC Avinguda Tibidabo)

Eating

Acontraluz

MEDITERRANEAN €€

6 MAP P148, B3

The most magical place to dine at this romantic restaurant is in the bougainvillea-draped, tree-filled garden, reached by an arbour. Olive-crusted monkfish with caramelised fennel, black paella with squid and clams, and suckling pig with fig jam are all outstanding choices. Don't miss the rum-soaked carrot cake with cardamom ice cream for dessert. (93 203 06 58; www.acontraluz.com; Carrer del Milanesat 19; mains €15-27; 1.30-4pm & 8.30pm-midnight Mon-Sat, 1.30-4pm Sun; FGC Les Tres Torres)

La Balsa

MEDITERRANEAN €€€

7 MAP P148, B2

With its grand ceiling and the scented gardens that surround the main terrace dining area, La Balsa is one of the city's premier dining addresses. The seasonally changing menu is a mix of traditional Catalan and creative expression (suckling pig with melon; cod confit with prune compote). Lounge over a cocktail at the bar before being directed to your table. (93 211 50 48; www.labalsarestaurant.com; Carrer de la Infanta Isabel 4; mains €20-28; 1.30-3.30pm & 8.30-10.30pm Tue-Sat, 1.30-3.30pm Sun; ; FGC Avinguda Tibidabo)

Mitja Vida

TAPAS €

8 MAP P148, D3

A young, fun, mostly local crowd gathers around the stainless-steel tapas bar of tiny Mitja Vida. It's a jovial eating and drinking spot, with good-sized portions of anchovies, calamari, smoked herring, cheeses and *mojama* (salt-cured tuna). The drink of choice is house-made vermouth. (www.morrofi.cat; Carrer de Brusi 39; tapas €3-7; 6-11pm Mon-Thu, noon-4pm & 6-11pm Fri & Sat, noon-4pm Sun, closed Aug; FGC Sant Gervasi)

Bar Tomàs

TAPAS €

9 MAP P148, B4

Many *barcelonins* swear Bar Tomàs is the best place in the city for *patatas bravas* (potato chunks) served with its house-speciality garlic aioli. Despite the fluorescent lights and low-key service, folks from all walks of life pile in, particularly for lunch on weekends. Fried artichokes, anchovies and other snacks also go nicely with an ice-cold beer. (93 203 10 77; www.eltomasdesarria.com; Carrer Major de Sarrià 49; tapas €2.50-7; noon-4pm & 6-10pm Mon-Sat; FGC Sarrià)

Vivanda

CATALAN **€€**

10 MAP P148, A3

With a menu designed by acclaimed Catalan chef Jordi Vilà, diners are in for a treat at this Sarrià classic. Changing dishes showcase seasonal fare, such as eggs with truffles, rice with cuttlefish, and artichokes with romesco sauce. Hidden behind the restaurant is the tree-shaded terrace with terracotta tiles and white-clothed tables. (93 203 19 18; www.vivanda.cat; Carrer Major de Sarrià 134; sharing plates €9-21; 1.30-3.30pm & 8.30-11pm Tue-Sat, 1.30-3.30pm Sun; FGC Reina Elisenda)

Bangkok Cafe

THAI **€€**

11 MAP P148, C5

If you're craving Thai cuisine, it's well worth making the trip out to Bangkok Cafe, which serves up spicy green papaya salad, *tam yam kung* (spicy prawn soup), crispy prawns with plum sauce, red curries and other standouts, with more spice than you'll find in most Catalan eateries. (93 339 32 69; Carrer d'Evarist Arnús 65; mains €10-14; 8-11pm Mon-Wed, 1-3.45pm & 8-11pm Thu-Sun; M Plaça del Centre)

A meal at Flash Flash (p152)

MATT MUNRO/LONELY PLANET ©

A Wander Through Old Sarrià

The old centre of Sarrià is a largely pedestrianised haven of peace. Probably founded in the 13th century and incorporated into Barcelona only in 1921, ancient Sarrià is formed around sinuous Carrer Major de Sarrià, today a mix of old and new, with a sprinkling of shops and restaurants.

At the street's top end is pretty **Plaça de Sarrià**. As you wander downhill, duck off into Plaça del Consell de la Vila, Plaça de Sant Vicenç de Sarrià and Carrer de Rocaberti, at the end of which is the Monestir de Santa Isabel, with a neo-Gothic cloister. Built in 1886 to house Clarissan nuns, it was abandoned during the civil war and used as an air-raid shelter.

5º Pino

CATALAN **€€**

12 MAP P148, B3

While exploring Sarrià, it's worth detouring a few blocks east to this charming cafe and restaurant, which is a favourite local spot for tasty sandwiches, salads, tortillas, tapas and drinks. It's on a busy road, though the outdoor pine-shaded terrace is still a pleasant spot for a bite. (Quinto Pino; 93 252 22 81; www.quintopino.es; Passeig de la Bonanova 98; sandwiches €8-13, tapas €1.50-7.50; kitchen 8.30am-midnight Mon-Fri, 10am-midnight Sat, bar to 1.30am; ; FGC Sarrià)

Hisop

MEDITERRANEAN **€€€**

13 MAP P148, D4

Black, white and burgundy dominate the dining room decor at this elegant little Michelin-starred eatery just off the beaten path. The seasonal menu is a work of art that might feature elderflower, fennel and grappa-marinated duck, grilled turbot with pistachio-stuffed jalapeño peppers and olive-oil-poached peach with carmelised ginger. (93 241 32 33; www.hisop.com; Passatge de Marimon 9; mains €24-28.50; 1.30-3.30pm & 8.30-11pm Mon-Fri, 8.30-11pm Sat; M Diagonal)

Flash Flash

SPANISH **€**

14 MAP P148, D4

Decorated with black-and-white murals and an all-white interior, Flash Flash has a fun and kitschy pop-art aesthetic that harks back to its opening in 1970. Fluffy tortillas are the speciality, with more than 50 varieties, as well as massive bunless hamburgers. (93 237 09 90; www.flashflashbarcelona.com; Carrer de la Granada del Penedès 25; dishes €6.30-13.80; 1pm-1.30am; ; FGC Gràcia)

Drinking

El Maravillas

COCKTAIL BAR

15 MAP P148, B5

Overlooking the peaceful Plaça de la Concòrdia, El Maravillas feels like a secret hideaway – especially if you've just arrived from the crowded lanes of the *Ciutat Vella* (Old City). The glittering bar has just a few tables, plus outdoor seating on the square in warm weather. Creative cocktails, good Spanish red wines and easy-drinking vermouths are the drinks of choice. (☎93 360 73 78; www.elmaravillas.cat; Plaça de la Concòrdia 15; ⊙noon-midnight Mon & Tue, to 1am Wed, to 2am Thu, to 3am Fri-Sun; Ⓜ Maria Cristina, T1, T2, T3 Numància)

Mirablau BAR

16 MAP P148, C1

Gaze out over the entire city from this privileged balcony restaurant at the base of the Funicular del Tibidabo. The bar is renowned for its gin selection, with 30 different varieties. Wander downstairs to join the folk in the tiny dance space, which opens at 11.30pm. In summer you can step out onto the even smaller terrace for a breather. (☎93 418 58 79; www.mirablaubcn.com; Plaça del Doctor Andreu; ⊙11am-3.30am Mon-Wed, 11am-4.30am Thu, 10am-5am Fri-Sat, 10am-2.30am Sun; 196, FGC Avinguda Tibidabo)

Marcel BAR

17 MAP P148, D4

A classic meeting place, Marcel has a homely, old-world feel, with a wood bar, black-and-white floor tiles and high windows. It offers snacks and tapas as well. Space is somewhat limited and customers inevitably spill out onto the footpath, where there are also a few tables. (☎93 209 89 48; Carrer de Santaló 42; ⊙7.30am-1am Mon-Thu, 7.30am-3am Fri & Sat, 9.30am-midnight Sun; FGC Muntaner)

Bikini CLUB

18 MAP P148, C4

This old star of the Barcelona nightlife scene has been keeping the beat since 1953. Every possible kind of music gets a run, from Latin and Brazilian beats to 1980s disco, depending on the night and the space you choose. (☎93 322 08 00; www.bikinibcn.com; Avinguda Diagonal 547; cover from €12; ⊙midnight-6am Thu-Sat; 6, 7, 33, 34, 63, 67, L51, L57, T1, T2, T3 L'Illa)

Entertainment

Luz de Gas LIVE MUSIC

19 MAP P148, D4

Several nights a week this club, set in a grand former theatre, stages concerts ranging through rock, soul, salsa, jazz and pop. Concerts typically kick off around 1am; from about 2am, the place turns into a club that attracts a well-dressed crowd with varying musical tastes, depending on the night. Check the website for the latest schedule. (☎93 209 77 11; www.luzdegas.com; Carrer de Muntaner 246; ⊙midnight-6am Thu-Sat; 6, 7, 27, 32, 33, 34, H8, T1, T2, T3 Francesc Macià)

Shopping

L'Illa Diagonal MALL

20 MAP P148, C4

One of Barcelona's best malls, this is a fine place to while away a few hours (or days), with high-end shops and a mesmerising spread of eateries. (☎93 444 00 00; www.lilla.com; Avinguda Diagonal 557; ⊙9.30am-9pm Mon-Sat; Ⓜ Maria Cristina)

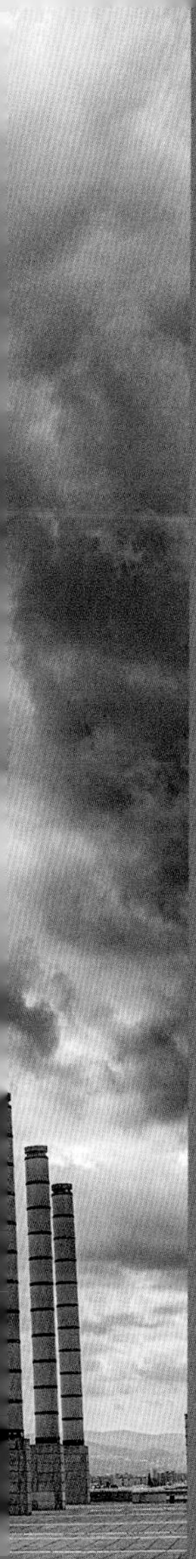

Explore

Montjuïc, Poble Sec & Sant Antoni

Montjuïc has some of the city's finest art collections: the Museu Nacional d'Art de Catalunya (MNAC), the Fundació Joan Miró and CaixaForum. Other galleries, gardens and an imposing castle form part of the scenery. Just below Montjuïc lie the lively tapas bars of Poble Sec, while the neighbourhood of Sant Antoni is currently the city's coolest.

Dining options on the hill are limited, so best to pack a picnic. We suggest you take the Teleférico del Puerto (p170) cable car from Barceloneta – start at the summit and work your way down. The Castell de Montjuïc (p170) has marvellous views, as do the nearby gardens. Visit the Fundació Joan Miró (p160) before finding a quiet corner of the Jardins de Mossèn Cinto de Verdaguer (p163) for lunch.

Take a peak at Barcelona's Olympic moment at L'Anella Olímpica & Estadi Olímpic (p170), then spend the rest of the afternoon exploring Catalan treasures at the renowned Museu Nacional d'Art de Catalunya (p156). Even if you don't have time to go inside, take a peak at CaixaForum (p168), housed in an eyecatching Modernista building.

Stay long enough to catch the Font Màgica (p168) before heading on to Quimet i Quimet (p171) for delicious tapas and end the night back up on Montjuïc with dancing at La Terrrazza (p173).

Getting There & Around

M Montjuïc's closest metro stops are Espanya, Poble Sec and Paral·lel.

Teleférico del Puerto from Torre de Sant Sebastiá in Barceloneta to Montjuïc.

Neighbourhood Map on p166

L'Anella Olímpica (p170) MARCO RUBINO/SHUTTERSTOCK ©

Top Sight

Museu Nacional d'Art de Catalunya

From across the city, the neobaroque silhouette of the Mirador del Palau Nacional can be seen on the slopes of Montjuïc. Built for the 1929 World Exhibition and restored in 2005, it houses a vast collection of mostly Catalan art spanning the early Middle Ages to the early 20th century. The highlight is the collection of extraordinary Romanesque frescoes.

MAP P166, C4

www.museunacional.cat

adult/child €12/free, after 3pm Sat & 1st Sun of month free

10am-8pm Tue-Sat, to 3pm Sun May-Sep, to 6pm Tue-Sat Oct-Apr

55, M Espanya

Romanesque Frescoes

The beautifully displayed Romanesque art section constitutes one of Europe's greatest such collections. It consists mainly of 11th- and 12th-century frescoes from churches in the Catalan Pyrenees. While it's all exceptional, the two outstanding collections are the Església de Sant Climent de Taüll frescoes (Room 7) and the Església de Santa Maria de Taüll frescoes (Room 9).

Gothic Collection

Lovers of medieval religious art will want to linger over the ground-floor display of Gothic art, which is dominated by deeply textured altarpieces and other works, including paintings by Catalan painters Bernat Martorell and Jaume Huguet. Amid it all, seek out the sculpture *Head of Christ* by Jaume Cascalls, a haunting bust dating from 1352.

El Greco & Fra Angelico

Before leaving the Gothic centuries and heading upstairs, two paintings warrant close and prolonged inspection. The first is Saint Peter and Saint Paul (1595–1600) by Doménikos Theotokópoulos, better known as El Greco. The second work is the *Madonna of Humility* (1433–35) by Fra Angelico, an idealised, near-perfect counterpoint to El Greco's slender, elongated figures.

Spanish Masters

After passing through the soaring auditorium, climb to the 1st floor, where the masters of 17th-century Spanish art make a brief appearance. Francisco de Zurbarán's *Immaculate Conception* (1632) looks out across Room 39 at his strangely disconcerting *Saint Francis of Assisi*. Nearby, Room 41 is shared by Josep de

★ Top Tips

- An audioguide costs €4.
- Be sure to take in the fine view from the **terrace** just in front of the museum. It draws crowds around sunset.
- Another fine viewpoint is on the museum's roof terrace (included in admission or €2 if you only want to visit the rooftop).

✕ Take a Break

There's a casual cafe on the main level for drinks, sandwiches and desserts. On the upper level, the beautifully set **Oleum** (☎ 93 289 06 79; www.oleumrestaurant.com; 1st floor, Museu Nacional d'Art de Catalunya (MNAC),; mains €14-21; ⊙12.30-4pm Tue-Thu & Sun, 12.30-4pm & 8.30-11pm Fri & Sat; 🚌 55, Ⓜ Espanya) serves high-end Mediterranean fare, with great views over the city.

Ribera and the masterful *Saint Paul* by Diego Velázquez (1619).

Catalan Masters

The 1st floor is dominated by Catalan painters and offers an intriguing insight into artists little known beyond Catalonia. There's much to turn the head, but our highlights are Mariano Fortuny's *La Batalla de Tetuan* (1863–73) and the works of Modernista painter Ramon Casas (1866–1932), especially *Ramon Casas and Pere Romeu on a Tandem* (1897).

Gaudí, Sorolla & Munch

Some furniture pieces by Antoni Gaudí and Joaquim Mir (1873–1940) continue the Catalan theme – the latter's *Terraced Village* (1909) is a lovely work. But dropped down amid this relatively uniform collection of Catalan art are two works by undoubted European masters: Valencian painter Joaquín Sorolla and Norwegian Edvard Munch.

Picasso & Dalí

Two sober works by Salvador Dalí – *Portrait of my Father* (1925) and *Portrait of Joan Maria Torres* (1921) – are what everyone comes to see, but fans of Picasso are rewarded by a handful of paintings, among them the cubist *Woman with Hat and Fur Collar* (1937), which is one of the museum's standout pieces.

Julio González

Having checked off the big names, most visitors head for the exit,

***Saint Francis of Assisi according to Pope Nicholas V's Vision*, by Francisco de Zurbarán**

but we recommend you stay long enough to appreciate the beautiful sculptures by Julio González (1876–1942), Catalonia's premier 20th-century sculptor. His abstract human forms, such as those in *Still Life II* (1929), have a slender grace.

Museu Nacional d'Art de Catalunya

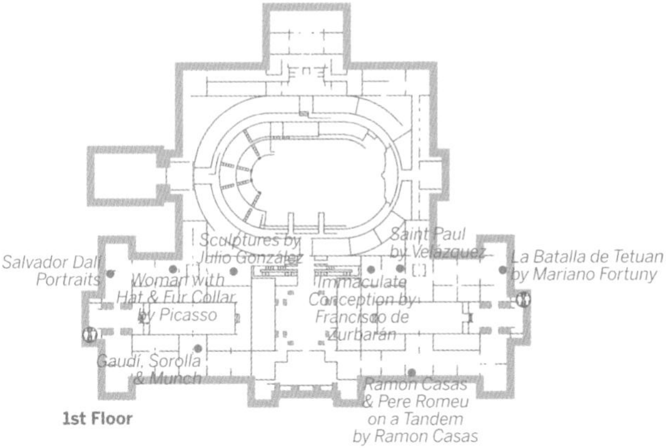

1st Floor

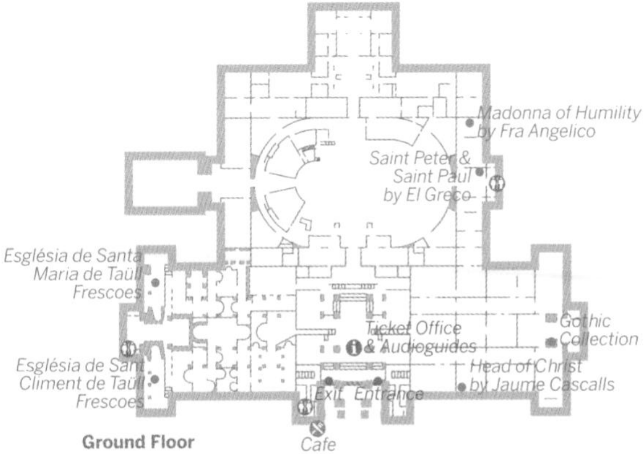

Ground Floor

Top Sight

Fundació Joan Miró

Dedicated to one of the greatest artists to emerge in Barcelona, Joan Miró (1893–1983), this outstanding gallery is a must-see. The foundation holds the greatest single collection of the artist's work, comprising around 220 of his paintings, 180 sculptures, some textiles and more than 8000 drawings. Only a smallish portion is ever on display, but there's always a representative sample from his early paintings through to a master in full command of his unique style.

MAP P166, E4

93 443 94 70

www.fmirobcn.org

Parc de Montjuïc

adult/child €12/free

10am-8pm Tue, Wed, Fri & Sat, to 9pm Thu, to 3pm Sun

55, 150, Paral·lel

The Formative Years

Room 16 The young Joan Miró began, like most masters, by painting figurative forms, but his move to Paris in 1920 prompted a shift to the avant-garde styles that he would make his own. His 1925 work *Painting (The White Glove)* has that unmistakable Miró sense of the artist having taken everything apart and reassembled it on a whim.

The War Years

Room 17 Miró spent most of the Spanish Civil War (1936–39) in exile in France, and his works from this period are uncharacteristically dark. During WWII, his approach to painting changed, reflecting a desire to escape reality, as highlighted in the bold colours and childlike figures of *The Morning Star* (1940) and *Woman Dreaming of Escape* (1945).

1960s & Paper

Rooms 19 & 20 After soaking up the vivid colours of Miró's 1960s paintings in Room 19 – linger over *Painting (for Emil Fernandez Miró)* from 1963 and *Catalan Peasant in the Moonlight* (1968) in particular – pause in Room 20. This is where Miró's love of painting on paper, and the flexibility it offered, is showcased with paintings that span five decades.

Col·lecció Katsuta

Rooms 21 & 22 This far-reaching private collection of Miró's works feels like an unexpected bonus at exhibition's end. It's a reprise of his career from the sober Catalan landscapes of his youth (such as *Landscape, Mont-Roig* in Room 21) through to the masterful and enigmatic *The Smile of a Tear* (1973) in Room 22.

★ Top Tips

- For the full experience, pay the extra €5 for the multimedia guide, which includes commentary on major works, additional info on Miro's life and work and images and photographs.
- Arrive at opening times for the smallest crowds.
- Head to the gardens just downhill from the museum for a scenic stroll after visiting the galleries.

✕ Take a Break

Near the centre of the museum, a light-filled restaurant serves freshly prepared Mediterranean dishes. The adjoining outdoor terrace is a fine spot for a drink.

A 250m walk southwest of the museum (head right when exiting), La Font del Gat (p163) has high-end Catalan cuisine with outdoor dining on the terrace.

Walking Tour

Views & Gardens on Montjuïc

Montjuïc, the hillside overlooking the port and across the city, is best explored on foot, along the numerous forest paths that zigzag through gardens and skirt the various sights.

Walk Facts

Start Castell de Montjuïc

End Jardins de Joan Maragall

Length 3km; 1½ hours

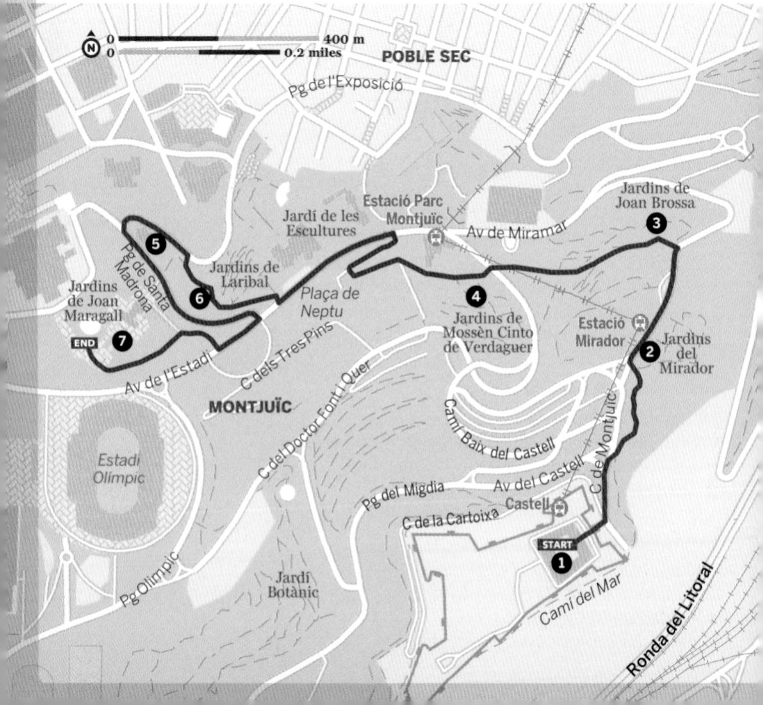

❶ Hilltop Castle

Long synonymous with oppression, the dark history of **Castell de Montjuïc** (p170) is today overshadowed by the stupendous views it commands over the city and sea. (Don't miss the little sea-facing trail behind the fortress.) The ride up on the Telefèric de Montjuïc is the perfect way to get here.

❷ Look-Out Point

A short stroll down the road or the parallel Camí del Mar pedestrian trail leads to another fine viewpoint overlooking the city and sea, the **Jardins del Mirador** (http://ajuntament.barcelona.cat/ecologiaurbana; Carretera de Montjuïc; admission free; 10am-sunset; Telefèric de Montjuïc, Mirador). Take the weight off on the park benches or pick up a snack.

❸ Celebrating the Sardana

Further downhill is the multitiered **Jardins de Joan Brossa** (Plaça de la Sardana; admission free; 10am-sunset; Telefèric de Montjuïc, Mirador). Enter on the left just beyond Plaça de la Sardana, which has a sculpture of people engaged in the classic Catalan folk dance. More fine city views can be had from among the many Mediterranean trees and plants.

❹ Tulips & Lilies

Exiting the Jardins de Joan Brossa on the western side, cross Camí Baix del Castell to the painstakingly laid out **Jardins de Mossèn Cinto de Verdaguer** (http://ajuntament.barcelona.cat/ecologiaurbana; Avinguda Miramar 30; admission free; 10am-sunset; 55, 150). This is a beautiful setting for a slow meander among tulip beds and water lilies.

❺ Alhambra-Inspired Terraces

Dropping away behind the Fundació Joan Miró, the 1922-established **Jardins de Laribal** (Passeig de Santa Madrona 2; admission free; 10am-sunset; 55) comprise a combination of terraced gardens linked by paths and stairways. The pretty sculpted watercourses along some of the stairways were inspired by Granada's palace of El Alhambra.

❻ A Lunch Stop

While in the gardens, you can take a break for a meal if hunger strikes. **La Font del Gat** (93 289 04 04; www.lafontdelgat.com; Passeig de Santa Madrona 28; 3-course menu €16; 10am-6pm Tue-Fri, noon-6pm Sat & Sun; 55) has a daily changing menu (no à la carte), and a lovely and spacious terrace dotted with orange trees and surrounded by greenery.

❼ Ornamental Gardens

Continue walking west, past the Estadi Olímpic (Olympic Stadium) to reach the lovely, but little visited **Jardins de Joan Maragall** (Avinguda dels Montanyans 48; admission free; 10am-3pm Sat & Sun; M Plaça Espanya). Lush lawns, ornamental fountains, photogenic sculptures and a neoclassical palace (the Spanish royal family's residence in Barcelona) set these gardens apart. The catch: the grounds are only open on weekends (10am to 3pm).

Walking Tour

Nightlife in Sant Antoni & Poble Sec

For locals, the area of Poble Sec and neighbouring Sant Antoni is the hot destination of the moment, with a buzzing array of cafes, bars and eateries drawing young, hip crowds to this once sleepy corner of Barcelona. This route starts off with some tapas bar snacking, before moving on to more serious drinking dens and nightspots.

Walk Facts

Start Bodega 1900

End Sala Apolo

Length 2.3km; all night

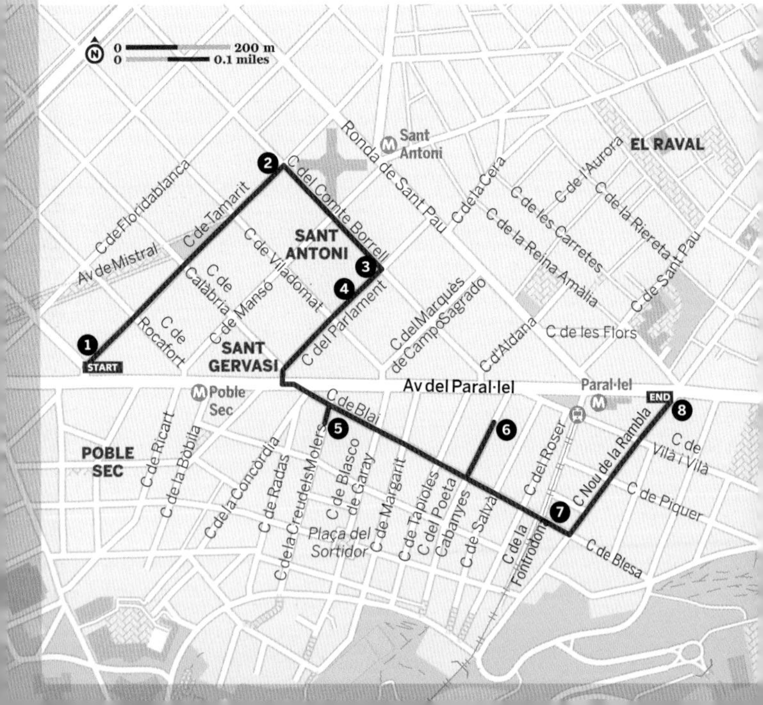

❶ Culinary Superstar

One of Albert Adrià's first-rate eating spots, **Bodega 1900** (p171) mimics an old-school tapas bar, but this is no ordinary joint. Witness, for example, the simply exquisite *mollete de calamars,* served piping hot from the oven with chipotle mayonnaise, kimchi and lemon zest.

❷ Tapas & Rock 'n' Roll

Near the Mercat de Sant Antoni, **Bar Ramón** (http://barramon.dudaone.com; Carrer del Comte Borrell 81; tapas €5-12; 8.30-11.30pm Mon-Thu, 9am-4pm & 8.30pm-midnight Fri & Sat) is a much-loved joint (opened in the 1930s) that serves superb tapas. Calamari, meatballs, stuffed mushrooms, octopus – you can't go wrong.

❸ Aussie Style

On a stretch that now teems with cafes, Australian-run **Federal** (www.federalcafe.es; Carrer del Parlament 39; mains €9-12; 8am-11pm Mon-Thu, 8am-1am Fri, 9am-1am Sat, 9am-5.30pm Sun;) was the trailbazer, with its breezy atmosphere and superb brunches. Alongside healthy, tasty meals, cupcakes and good coffee are available all day. The leafy roof terrace is a pleasant spot.

❹ Terrace Drinks

It bills itself as a wine bar, but actually the wine selection at **Bar Calders** (Carrer del Parlament 25; 5pm-2am Mon-Fri, 11am-2.30am Sat, 11am-12.30am Sun) is its weak point. As an all-day cafe and tapas bar, however, it's unbeatable. With a few tables outside on a tiny pedestrian side-street, this is the favoured meeting point for the neighbourhood's boho element.

❺ Atmospheric Den

A succession of nooks and crannies, dotted with flea-market finds and dimly lit in violets, reds and yellows, **Tinta Roja** (www.tintaroja.cat; Carrer de la Creu dels Molers 17; 8.30pm-12.30am Wed, to 2am Thu, to 3am Fri & Sat, closed Aug) is an intimate spot for a drink and an occasional show.

❻ Air of Decadence

Seduction is the word that springs to mind in **El Rouge** (Carrer del Poeta Cabanyes 21; 9pm-2am Thu, 10pm-3am Fri & Sat, 11am-2am Sun;), a bordello-red lounge cocktail bar. The walls are laden with heavy-framed paintings, dim lamps and mirrors, and no two chairs are alike. It also hosts poetry readings, theatrical shows, art exhibitions.

❼ Bohemian Bodega

At **Gran Bodega Saltó** (www.bodegasalto.net; Carrer de Blesa 36; 7pm-2am Mon-Thu, noon-3am Fri & Sat, noon-midnight Sun) the barrels give away the bar's history as a traditional bodega. Now, after a little psychedelic redecoration with odd lamps, figurines and old Chinese beer ads, it's a magnet for an eclectic barfly crowd that can get pretty lively on nights when there is live music.

❽ Dancehall Finale

The iconic **Sala Apolo** (93 441 40 01; www.sala-apolo.com; Carrer Nou de la Rambla 113; club from €15, concerts vary; concerts from 8pm, club from midnight) is a fine old dancehall, where red velvet dominates and you feel as though you're on a movie set. There are concerts earlier in the evening, with DJs after midnight.

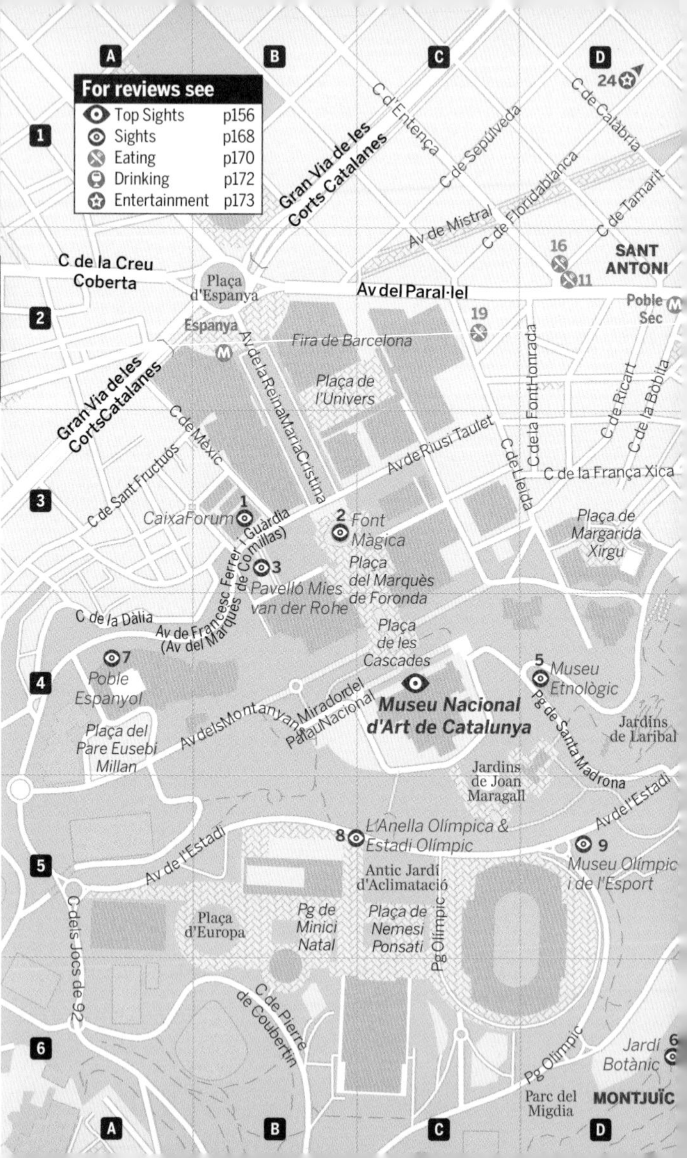
For reviews see
Top Sights p156
Sights p168
Eating p170
Drinking p172
Entertainment p173
A
B
C
D
1
2
3
4
5
6
Gran Via de les Corts Catalanes
C d'Entença
C de Sepúlveda
C de Calàbria
C de Floridablanca
C de Tamarit
Av de Mistral
24
16
11
SANT ANTONI
C de la Creu Coberta
Plaça d'Espanya
Av del Paral·lel
Poble Sec
19
Espanya
Fira de Barcelona
Av de la Reina Maria Cristina
Plaça de l'Univers
C de la Font Honrada
C de Ricart
C de la Bobila
C de Mèxic
C de Sant Fructuós
Av de Rius i Taulet
C de Lleida
C de la França Xica
1
CaixaForum
2
Font Màgica
Plaça de Margarida Xirgu
C Guàrdia i Ferrer (C de Comillas)
3
Pavelló Mies van der Rohe
Plaça del Marquès de Foronda
C de la Dàlia
Av de Francesc Ferrer i Guàrdia (Av del Marquès de Comillas)
Plaça de les Cascades
7
Poble Espanyol
5
Museu Etnològic
Mirador del Palau Nacional
Museu Nacional d'Art de Catalunya
Av dels Montanyans
Pg de Santa Madrona
Jardins de Laribal
Plaça del Pare Eusebi Millan
Jardins de Joan Maragall
Av de l'Estadi
8
L'Anella Olímpica & Estadi Olímpic
9
Museu Olímpic i de l'Esport
Antic Jardí d'Aclimatació
C dels Jocs de 92
Plaça d'Europa
Pg de Minici Natal
Plaça de Nemesi Ponsati
Pg Olímpic
C de Pierre de Coubertin
Jardí Botànic
6
Parc del Migdia
MONTJUÏC

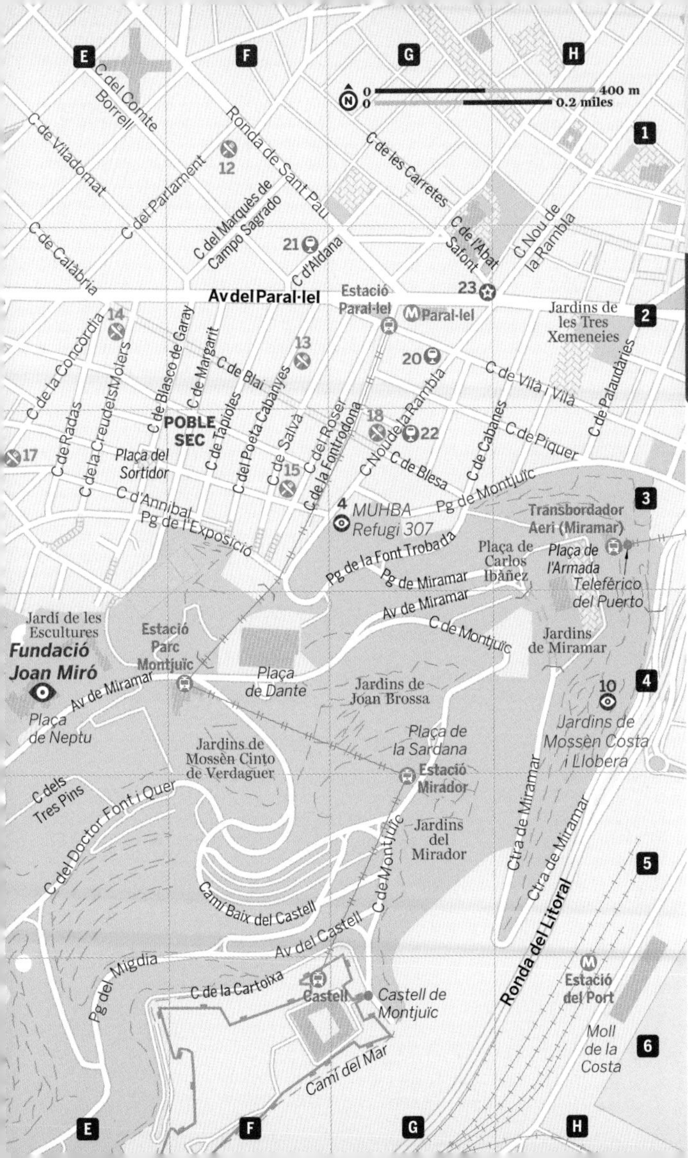
E
F
G
H
1
2
3
4
5
6
0
400 m
0
0.2 miles
C del Comte Borrell
C de Viladomat
Ronda de Sant Pau
C del Parlament
C del Marquès de Campo Sagrado
C de les Carretes
C de Calàbria
C d'Aldana
C de l'Abat Safont
C Nou de la Rambla
Av del Paral·lel
Estació Paral·lel
Paral·lel
Jardins de les Tres Xemeneies
C de la Concòrdia
C de la Creu dels Molers
C de Blasco de Garay
C de Margarit
C de Blai
C del Poeta Cabanyes
C de Vilà i Vilà
C de Palaudàries
C de Radas
POBLE SEC
C de Tapioles
C de Salvà
C del Roser
C de la Fontrodona
C Nou de la Rambla
C de Cabanes
C de Piquer
Plaça del Sortidor
C de Blesa
C d'Annibal
Pg de Montjuïc
Pg de l'Exposició
MUHBA Refugi 307
Transbordador Aeri (Miramar)
Pg de la Font Trobada
Plaça de Carlos Ibáñez
Plaça de l'Armada
Pg de Miramar
Av de Miramar
Teleférico del Puerto
Jardí de les Escultures
Fundació Joan Miró
Estació Parc Montjuïc
C de Montjuïc
Jardins de Miramar
Plaça de Dante
Jardins de Joan Brossa
Av de Miramar
Plaça de Neptu
Jardins de Mossèn Costa i Llobera
Plaça de la Sardana
Jardins de Mossèn Cinto de Verdaguer
Estació Mirador
C dels Tres Pins
C del Doctor Font i Quer
Jardins del Mirador
C de Montjuïc
Ctra de Miramar
Ctra de Miramar
Camí Baix del Castell
Av del Castell
Ronda del Litoral
Pg del Migdia
C de la Cartoixa
Castell
Castell de Montjuïc
Estació del Port
Moll de la Costa
Camí del Mar
12
21
23
14
13
20
18
22
17
15
4
10

Sights

CaixaForum GALLERY

1 MAP P166, B3

The Caixa building society prides itself on its involvement in (and ownership of) art, in particular all that is contemporary. Its premier art expo space in Barcelona hosts part of the bank's extensive collection from around the globe. The setting is a completely renovated former factory, the Fàbrica Casaramona, an outstanding Modernista brick structure designed by Puig i Cadafalch. From 1940 to 1993 it housed the First Squadron of the police cavalry unit – 120 horses in all. (93 476 86 00; www.caixaforum.es; Avinguda de Francesc Ferrer i Guàrdia 6-8; adult/child €4/free, 1st Sun of month free; 10am-8pm; M Espanya)

Font Màgica FOUNTAIN

2 MAP P166, B3

A huge fountain that crowns the long sweep of the Avinguda de la Reina Maria Cristina to the grand facade of the Palau Nacional, Font Màgica is a unique performance in which the water can look like seething fireworks or a mystical cauldron of colour. (93 316 10 00; Avinguda de la Reina Maria Cristina; admission free; every 30min 7.30-10.30pm Wed-Sun Jun-Sep, 9-10pm Thu-Sat Apr, May & Oct, 8-9pm Thu-Sat Nov-early Jan & mid-Feb–Mar; M Espanya)

Pavelló Mies van der Rohe ARCHITECTURE

3 MAP P166, B3

The Pavelló Mies van der Rohe is a work of artful simplicity that is emblematic of the Modernisme movement. The structure has been the subject of many studies and interpretations, and it has inspired several generations of architects. That said, unless you're an avid architecture fan, there isn't much to see inside beyond what you can glean from the building's exterior. (93 215 10 11; www.miesbcn.com; Avinguda de Francesc Ferrer i Guàrdia 7; adult/child €5/free; 10am-8pm Mar-Oct, 10am-6pm Nov-Feb; M Espanya)

MUHBA Refugi 307 HISTORIC SITE

4 MAP P166, G3

Part of the Museu d'Història de Barcelona (MUHBA), this shelter dates back to the days of the Spanish Civil War. Barcelona was the city most heavily bombed from the air during the war and had more than 1300 air-raid shelters. Local citizens started digging this one under a fold of Montjuïc in March 1937. Compulsory tours are conducted in English at 10.30am, Spanish at 11.30am and Catalan at 12.30pm on Sundays. Reserve ahead as places are limited. (93 256 21 22; http://ajuntament.barcelona.cat/museuhistoria; Carrer Nou de la Rambla 175; adult/child incl tour €3.40/free; tours in English 10.30am Sun; M Paral·lel)

Museu Etnològic MUSEUM

5 MAP P166, D4

Barcelona's ethnology museum presents an intriguing permanent collection that delves into the rich heritage of Catalonia. Exhibits cover origin myths, religious festivals, folklore, and the blending of the sacred and the secular (along those lines, don't miss the Nativity scene with that quirky Catalan character *el caganer,* aka 'the crapper'). (☎93 424 68 07; http://ajuntament.barcelona.cat/museuetnologic; Passeig de Santa Madrona 16-22; adult/child €5/free, 4-8pm Sun & 1st Sun of month free; ⏰10am-7pm Tue-Sat, to 8pm Sun; 🚌55)

Jardí Botànic GARDENS

6 MAP P166, D6

This botanical garden is dedicated to Mediterranean flora and has a collection of some 40,000 plants and 1500 species, including many that thrive in areas with a climate similar to that of the Mediterranean, such as the Canary Islands, North Africa, Australia, California, Chile and South Africa. (www.museuciencies.cat; Carrer del Doctor Font i Quer 2; adult/child €3.50/free, after 3pm Sun & 1st Sun of month free; ⏰10am-7pm Apr-Sep, to 5pm Oct-Mar; 🚌55, 150)

Poble Espanyol CULTURAL CENTRE

7 MAP P166, A4

Welcome to Spain! All of it! This 'Spanish Village' is an intriguing scrapbook of Spanish architecture built for the Spanish crafts section of the 1929 World Exhibition. You can meander from Andalucía to the Balearic Islands in the space of a couple of hours, visiting surprisingly good copies of Spain's characteristic structures. The 117 buildings include 17 restaurants, cafes and bars – including **La Terrrazza** (☎687 969825; www.laterrrazza.com; cover from €15; ⏰midnight-6.30am Thu-Sat May-Sep) – and 20 craft shops and workshops (for glass artists and other artisans), as well as souvenir stores. (www.poble-espanyol.com; Avinguda de Francesc Ferrer i Guàrdia 13; adult/child €14/7; ⏰9am-8pm Mon, to midnight Tue-Thu & Sun, to 3am Fri, to 4am Sat; 🚌13, 23, 150, Ⓜ Espanya)

Pavelló Mies van der Rohe

Travel By Cable Car

The fastest way to get from Barceloneta to Montjuïc is aboard the **Teleférico del Puerto** (p179), which offers sublime views of sea and city. On Montjuïc, another cable car, the **Telefèric de Montjuïc** (p179), runs from Estació Parc Montjuïc to the **Castell de Montjuïc** (Map p166, G6; 93 256 44 45; http://ajuntament.barcelona.cat/castelldemontjuic; Carretera de Montjuïc 66; adult/child €5/3, after 3pm Sun & 1st Sun of month free; 10am-8pm Apr-Oct, to 6pm Nov-Mar; 150, Telefèric de Montjuïc, Castell de Montjuïc).

L'Anella Olímpica & Estadi Olímpic

AREA

8 MAP P166, B5

L'Anella Olímpica (Olympic Ring) is the group of installations built for the main events of the 1992 Olympics. They include the **Piscines Bernat Picornell** (93 423 40 41; www.picornell.cat; Avinguda de l'Estadi 30-38; adult/child €11.90/7.30, nudist hours €6.55/4.70; 6.45am-midnight Mon-Fri, 7am-9pm Sat, 7.30am-4pm Sun; 13, 150), where the swimming and diving events were held, and the **Estadi Olímpic** (93 426 20 89; www.estadiolimpic.cat; Passeig Olímpic 15-17; admission free; 8am-8pm May-Sep, 10am-6pm Oct-Apr; 13, 150), which is open to the public when it's not in use for sporting events or concerts. (www.estadiolimpic.cat; Avinguda de l'Estadi; admission free; 13, 150)

Museu Olímpic i de l'Esport

MUSEUM

9 MAP P166, D5

The Museu Olímpic i de l'Esport is an information-packed interactive sporting museum. After picking up tickets, you wander down a ramp that snakes below ground level and is lined with multimedia displays on the history of sport and the Olympic Games, starting with the ancients. (93 292 53 79; www.museuolimpicbcn.cat; Avinguda de l'Estadi 60; adult/child €5.80/free; 10am-8pm Tue-Sat, to 2.30pm Sun Apr-Sep, 10am-6pm Tue-Sat, to 2.30pm Sun Oct-Mar; 55, 150)

Jardins de Mossèn Costa i Llobera

GARDENS

10 MAP P166, H4

Above the thundering traffic of the main road to Tarragona, the Jardins de Mossèn Costa i Llobera have a good collection of tropical and desert plants – including a veritable forest of cacti (Europe's largest collection), with some species reaching over 5m in height. (http://ajuntament.barcelona.cat/ecologiaurbana; Carretera de Miramar 38; admission free; 10am-sunset; Transbordador Aeri, Miramar)

Eating

Tickets

TAPAS, GASTRONOMY **€€€**

11 MAP P166, D2

A flamboyant affair playing with circus images and theatre lights, this is one of the sizzling tickets in the restaurant world, a Michelin-starred tapas bar opened by Ferran Adrià, of the legendary (since closed) El Bulli, and his brother Albert. Bookings are only taken online two months in advance, but you can try calling for last-minute cancellations. (☎93 292 42 50; www.ticketsbar.es; Avinguda del Paral·lel 164; tapas €3-26; ⊙7-11.30pm Tue-Fri, 1-3.30pm & 7-11.30pm Sat, closed Aug; MParal·lel)

Agust Gastrobar

BISTRO €€

12 MAP P166, F1

Set up by two French chefs (one of whom trained under Gordon Ramsay), Agust occupies a fabulous mezzanine space with timber beams, exposed brick and textured metro tiles. Baby scallops with seaweed butter and prawn-stuffed avocado cannelloni are savoury standouts; desserts include the extraordinary 'el cactus' (chocolate-crumble soil, mojito mousse and prickly pear sorbet) served in a terracotta flower pot. (☎93 162 67 33; www.agustbarcelona.com; Carrer del Parlament 54; mains €12.50-24; ⊙kitchen 7pm-midnight Mon-Thu, 2pm-midnight Fri-Sun, bar to 2am; MPoble Sec)

Quimet i Quimet

TAPAS €€

13 MAP P166, F2

Quimet i Quimet is a family-run business that has been passed down from generation to generation. There's barely space to swing a *calamar* (squid) in this bottle-lined, standing-room-only place, but it is a treat for the palate, with *montaditos* (tapas on a slice of bread) made to order. (☎93 442 31 42; Carrer del Poeta Cabanyes 25; tapas €4-10, montaditos €2.80-4; ⊙noon-4pm & 7-10.30pm Mon-Fri, noon-4pm Sat, closed Aug; MParal·lel)

Mano Rota

BISTRO €€

14 MAP P166, E2

Exposed brick, aluminium pipes, industrial light fittings and recycled timbers create a hip, contemporary setting for inspired bistro cooking at Mano Rota (which literally translates as 'broken hand', but is actually a Spanish idiom for consummate skill). Asian, South American and Mediterranean flavours combine in dishes such as crispy squid with yuzu aioli or dorade (bream) with pak choy pesto. (☎93 164 80 41; www.manorota.com; Carrer de la Creu dels Molers 4; mains €15-22; ⊙8-11.30pm Mon, 1-3.30pm & 8-11.30pm Tue-Sat, 1-3.30pm Sun; MPoble Sec)

Lascar 74

PERUVIAN €€

15 MAP P166, F3

At this self-styled 'ceviche and pisco bar', oyster shooters with leche de tigre (the traditional ceviche marinade) are served alongside exquisite Peruvian ceviches as well as renditions from Thailand, Japan and Mexico. Pisco sours are the real deal, frothy egg white and all. (☎93 017 98 72; www.lascar.es; Carrer del Roser 74; mains €12-15; ⊙7-11.30pm Mon-Thu, 2-5pm & 7pm-11.30pm Fri-Sun; MParal·lel)

Bodega 1900

TAPAS €€

16 MAP P166, D2

Bodega 1900 mimics an old-school tapas and vermouth bar, but don't be fooled: this venture from the world-famous Adrià brothers creates gastronomic tapas such as 'spherified' reconstructed olives, or its *mollete de calamars*, probably the best squid sandwich in the world, hot from the pan and served with chipotle mayonnaise, kimchi and lemon zest. (93 325 26 59; www.bodega1900.com; Carrer de Tamarit 91; tapas €6-15; 1pm-10.30pm Tue-Sat, closed Aug; M Poble Sec)

Casa Xica FUSION €€

17 MAP P166, E3

On the parlour floor of an old house, Casa Xica is a casual but artfully designed space where elements of the Far East are fused with fresh Catalan ingredients (owners Marc and Raquel lived and travelled in Asia). (93 600 58 58; Carrer de la França Xica 20; sharing plates €5-15; 8.30-11pm Mon, 1.30-11pm Tue-Sat; M Poble Sec)

Palo Cortao TAPAS €€

18 MAP P166, G3

Contemporary Palo Cortao is renowned for its beautifully executed seafood and meat dishes, served at fair prices. Highlights include roast oxtail with vermouth jus, octopus with white bean hummus, smoked mackerel with pickled jalapeño and tuna tataki tempura. Its long wooden bar with metal stools is ideal for solo diners. (93 188 90 67; www.palocortao.es; Carrer de Nou de la Rambla 146; mains €10-15; 8pm-1am Tue-Fri, 1-5pm & 8pm-1am Sat & Sun; M Paral·lel)

Casa de Tapas Cañota TAPAS €€

19 MAP P166, C2

Between Poble Sec and Plaça d'Espanya, this friendly, unfussy option serves affordable, nicely turned out tapas plates. Seafood is the speciality, with rich razor clams, garlic-fried prawns and tender octopus. Wash it down with a refreshing bottle of *albariño* (a Galician white). (93 325 91 71; www.casadetapas.com; Carrer de Lleida 7; tapas €5-14; 1-4pm & 7.30pm-midnight Tue-Sat, 1-4pm Sun; M Poble Sec)

Drinking

Abirradero BREWERY

20 MAP P166, G2

Barcelona is spoilt for choice with craft breweries, and this bright, buzzing space has 20 of its own beers rotating on the taps, including IPAral·lel (a double IPA), Excuse Me While I Kiss My Stout, and Tripel du Poble Sec. Tapas, sharing boards and burgers are standouts from the kitchen. You'll occasionally catch live jazz and blues here. (93 461 94 46; www.abirradero.com; Carrer Vila i Vilà 77; 5pm-1am Mon-Thu, noon-2am Fri & Sat, noon-1am Sun; ; M Paral·lel)

Bar Olimpia BAR

21 MAP P166, F2

This great little neighbourhood bar is a small slice of Barcelona history. It was here (and on the surrounding block), where the popular Olimpia Theatre Circus performed between 1924 and 1947. Today the retro setting draws a diverse crowd, who come for house-made vermouth, snacks (like quesadillas, cheese platters and tuna tartare) and strong gin and tonics. (676 828232; Carrer d'Aldana 11; 5pm-1am Mon-Wed, 5pm-2am Thu, 5pm-3am Fri, 1pm-3am Sat, 1pm-1am Sun; M Paral·lel)

Sala Plataforma

CLUB

22 MAP P166, G3

With two adjoining if smallish dance spaces, 'Platform' feels like a clandestine location in an otherwise quiet residential street. Inside this friendly, straightforward dance dive, you'll find popular '80s grooves, timeless rock and occasional live bands – plus drum and bass. (93 329 00 29; www.salaplataforma.com; Carrer Nou de la Rambla 145; cover from €6; 10pm-6am Thu-Sat, 7pm-2am Sun; M Paral·lel)

Entertainment

BARTS

CONCERT VENUE

23 MAP P166, G2

BARTS has a solid reputation for its innovative line-up of urban dance troupes, electro swing, psychedelic pop and other eclectic fare. Its smart design combines a comfortable midsized auditorium with excellent acoustics. Hours and ticket prices vary; check the agenda online. (Barcelona Arts on Stage; 93 324 84 92; www.barts.cat; Avinguda del Paral·lel 62; M Paral·lel)

Renoir Floridablanca

CINEMA

24 MAP P166, D1

With seven screens, this cinema shows a mix of quality art-house flicks and blockbusters in their original language (with Spanish subtitles). It's handily located just beyond El Raval, so you'll find no shortage of post-film entertainment options nearby. (91 542 27 02; www.cinesrenoir.com; Carrer de Floridablanca 135; M Sant Antoni)

Quimet i Quimet (p171)

tida La Rambla - Teatre Liceu
14, 38, 59
ceu
M

Survival Guide

A Barcelona metro station PHILIPUS/ALAMY STOCK PHOTO ©

Before You Go

Book Your Stay

- Accommodation in Barcelona is at a premium year-round so always book as far in advance as possible.
- Barcelona's price-to-quality ratio is generally high, but prices can double on weekends and during important festivals and trade fairs.
- Staying in the Barri Gòtic, El Raval or La Ribera puts you in the heart of the action, but nights can be noisy and long from Thursday through the weekend.
- L'Eixample can be quieter (assuming you're not on a busy boulevard), while Barceloneta is perfect if you're here for the beach.

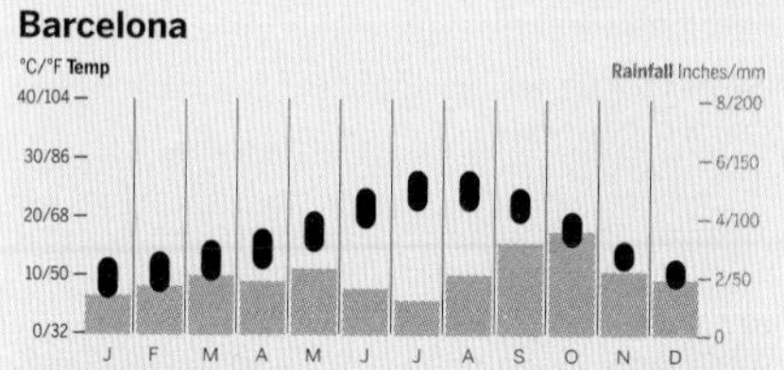

When to Go

- **Summer (Jun–Aug)** Hot beach weather, but often overwhelmed with visitors in July and August; locals escape in August.
- **Autumn (Sep–Nov)** September is one of the best months to visit; chance of rain in October and November.
- **Winter (Dec–Feb)** Nights can be chilly and there's a chance of rain, but there are fewer visitors and sunny days are possible.
- **Spring (Mar–May)** A lovely time to visit. Manageable visitor numbers, though rain is possible in April and May.

Useful Websites

Lonely Planet (www.lonelyplanet.com/barcelona) Neighbourhood profiles, plus extensive listings of hotels, hostels, guesthouses and apartments.

Oh Barcelona (www.oh-barcelona.com) Hotel and apartment listings, plus tips on deciding where to stay.

Barcelona Bed and Breakfasts (www.barcelonabedandbreakfasts.com) Listings of low-key, oft-overlooked lodging options.

Best Budget

Casa Gràcia (www.casagraciabcn.com) Stylish hostel with colourful rooms, communal dinners, film screenings and other events.

Pensió 2000 (www.pensio2000.com) Family-run pensión looking over the Palau de la Música.

Pars Tailor's Hostel (www.parshostels.com) A hip Sant Antoni option with a vintage vibe.

Pars Teatro Hostel (www.parshostels.com) Theatrically decorated space on the edge of Poble Sec.

Best Midrange

Five Rooms (www.thefiverooms.com) Small and charming with beautifully designed rooms.

Barceló Raval (www.thefiverooms.com) Hotel with design smarts and an appealing rooftop terrace.

Hotel Market (www.hotelmarketbarcelona.com) Beautifully designed rooms in the very hot 'hood of Sant Antoni.

Grand Hotel Central (www.grandhotelcentral.com) Simply the most stunning pool in town.

Best Top End

Soho House (www.sohohousebarcelona.com) Outpost of the London member's club, with every comfort.

Hotel Neri (www.hotelneri.com) Beautiful, historic hotel on a tranquil spot in Barri Gòtic.

Hotel Mercer (www.mercerbarcelona.com) Peaceful retreat with medieval details and atmospheric rooms.

Hotel Majéstic (www.hotelmajestic.es) A grand dame of L'Eixample.

Arriving in Barcelona

El Prat Airport

Barcelona's **El Prat airport** (☎902 404704; www.aena.es) lies 17km southwest of Plaça de Catalunya at El Prat de Llobregat. The airport has two main terminal buildings: the T1 terminal and the older T2, itself divided into three terminal areas (A, B and C). The main **tourist office** (www.barcelonaturisme.com; ⌚8.30am-8.30pm) is on the ground floor of Terminal 2B. Others on the ground floor of Terminal 2A and in Terminal 1 operate the same hours.

- The **Aerobús** (☎902 100104; www.aerobusbcn.com; Plaça d'Espanya; one way/return €5.90/10.20; ⌚5.05am-12.35am) runs from both terminals to Plaça de Catalunya (30 to 40 minutes depending on traffic) via Plaça d'Espanya, Gran Via de les Corts Catalanes (corner of Carrer del Comte d'Urgell) and Plaça de la Universitat every five to 10 minutes from 6.10am to 1.05am. Departures from Plaça de Catalunya are from 5.30am to 12.30am and stop at the corner of Carrer de Sepúlveda and Carrer del Comte d'Urgell, and at Plaça d'Espanya.
- R2 Nord line every half-hour from the airport (from 5.42am to 11.38pm) via several stops to Barcelona's main train station, Estació Sants, and Passeig de Gràcia.The trip between the airport and Passeig de Gràcia takes 25 minutes. A one-way ticket costs €2.50. The airport train station is about a five-minute walk from Terminal 2.
- A taxi between either terminal and the city centre – about a half-hour ride depending on traffic – costs around €25.

Estació de Sants

The main train station in Barcelona is **Estació Sants** (www.adif.es; Plaça dels Països Catalans; Ⓜ Sants Estació), located 2.5km west of La Rambla. Direct overnight trains from Paris, Geneva, Milan and Zurich arrive here. From here it's a short metro ride to the centre. The station has a **tourist office** (8am-8pm; Sants Estació), a telephone and fax office, currency exchange booths open between 8am and 10pm, ATMs and **left-luggage lockers** (left-luggage lockers; €3-5 per day; 24hr).

Estació del Nord

Barcelona's long-haul **bus station** (93 706 53 66; www.barcelonanord.cat; Carrer d'Ali Bei 80; Arc de Triomf) is located in L'Eixample, about 1.5km northeast of Plaça de Catalunya, and is a short walk from the Arc de Triomf metro station.

Getting Around

Metro

The easy-to-use metro system has 11 numbered and colour-coded lines. It runs from 5am to midnight Sunday to Thursday and holidays, from 5am to 2am on Friday and days immediately preceding holidays, and 24 hours on Saturday.

Bus

Transports Metropolitans de Barcelona (TMB; 93 298 70 00; www.tmb.net) buses run along most city routes every few minutes from between 5am and 6.30am to around 10pm and 11pm. Many routes pass through Plaça de Catalunya and/or Plaça de la Universitat.

After 11pm a reduced network of yellow nitbusos (night buses) runs until 3am or 5am. All nitbus routes pass through Plaça de Catalunya and most run every 30 to 45 minutes.

FGC Trains

Suburban trains run by the **Ferrocarrils de la Generalitat de Catalunya** (FGC; 012; www.fgc.net) include a couple of useful city lines. All lines heading north from Plaça de Catalunya stop at Carrer de Provença and Gràcia. One of these lines (L7) goes to Tibidabo and another (L6 to Reina Elisenda) has a stop near the Monestir de Pedralbes. Most trains from Plaça de Catalunya continue beyond Barcelona to Sant Cugat, Sabadell and Terrassa. Other FGC lines head west from Plaça d'Espanya, including one for Manresa that is handy for the trip to Montserrat.

Taxi

Taxis charge €2.10 flag fall plus meter charges of €1.10 per kilometre (€1.30 from 8pm to 8am and all day on weekends). A further €3.10 is added for all trips to/from the airport, and €1 for luggage bigger than 55cm x 35cm x 35cm. The trip from Estació Sants to Plaça de Catalunya, about 3km, costs about €11.

Bicycle

- Barcelona has over 180km of bike lanes.
- A waterfront path runs northeast from Barceloneta to Port Olímpic and onwards to Riu Besòs.
- There are numerous places to hire bikes, particularly in the Barri Gòtic and La

Ribera. Note that the red 'Bicing' hire bikes are available for Barcelona residents only.

- You can transport your bicycle on the metro on weekdays (except between 7am and 9.30am, and 5pm and 8.30pm). On weekends, holidays, and during July and August, there are no restrictions.

Cable Car

Teleférico del Puerto (93 430 47 16; www.telefericodebarcelona.com; Avinguda de Miramar; one way/return €11/16.50; 10.30am-8pm Jun–mid-Sep, 10.30am-7pm Mar-May & mid-Sep–Oct, 11am-5.30pm Nov-Feb; 150) Travels between the waterfront southwest of Barceloneta and Montjuïc.

Telefèric de Montjuïc (93 328 90 03; www.telefericdemontjuic.cat; Avinguda de Miramar 30; adult/child one way €8.20/6.50; 10am-9pm Jun-Sep, 10am-7pm Mar-May & Oct, 10am-6pm Nov-Feb; 55, 150) Runs between Estació Parc Montjuïc and the Castell de Montjuïc.The two cable-car stations are roughly 1.3km from each other. You can also reach the Telefèric de Montjuïc via the funicular railway that runs from the metro at the Paral·lel stop and is part of the metro fare system.

Essential Information

Business Hours

Standard opening hours are as follows:

Banks 8.30am to 2pm Monday to Friday; some also 4pm to 7pm Thursday or 9am to 1pm Saturday

Bars 6pm to 2am (to 3am weekends)

Clubs Midnight to 6am Thursday to Saturday

Department stores 10am to 10pm Monday to Saturday

Museums & art galleries Vary considerably; generally 10am to 8pm (some shut for lunch around 2pm to 4pm). Many close all day Monday and from 2pm Sunday.

Restaurants 1pm to 4pm and 8.30pm to midnight

Shops 9am or 10am to 1.30pm or 2pm and 4pm or 4.30pm to 8pm or 8.30pm Monday to Saturday

Discount Cards

Articket (www.articketbcn.org) gives admission to six sites for €30 and is valid for six months. You can pick up the ticket at the tourist offices at Plaça de Catalunya, Plaça de Sant Jaume and Estació Sants train station and at the museums themselves. The six sights are:

- Museu Picasso (p74)
- Museu Nacional d'Art de Catalunya (p156)
- MACBA (p65)
- Fundació Antoni Tàpies (p114)
- Centre de Cultura Contemporània de Barcelona (p66)
- Fundació Joan Miró(p160)

Arqueoticket is for those with an interest in archaeology and ancient history. The ticket (€14.50) is available from participating museums and tourist offices and grants free admission to the following sites:

o **Museu d'Arqueologia de Catalunya** (MAC; ☎93 423 21 49; www.mac.cat; Passeig de Santa Madrona 39-41; adult/child €5.50/free; ⏰9.30am-7pm Tue-Sat, 10am-2.30pm Sun; 🚌55, Ⓜ Poble Sec)

o Museu Egipci (p115)

o Museu d'Història de Barcelona (p52)

o Born Centre de Cultura i Memòria (p85)

Barcelona Card (www.barcelonacard.com) is handy if you want to see lots in a limited time. It costs €20/45/55/60 for two/three/four/five days. You get free transport, discounted admission (up to 60% off) or free entry to many museums and other sights, and minor discounts on purchases at a small number of shops, restaurants and bars. The card costs about 50% less for children aged four to 12. You can purchase it at tourist offices and online (buying online saves you 5%).

The **Ruta del Modernisme** (www.rutadelmodernisme.com) pack costs €12 and is well worth looking into for visiting Modernista sights at discounted rates.

Electricity

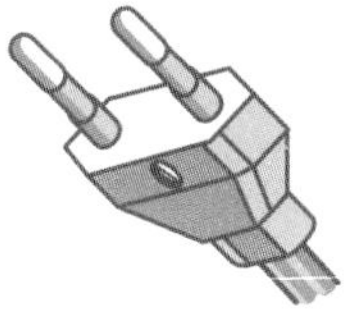

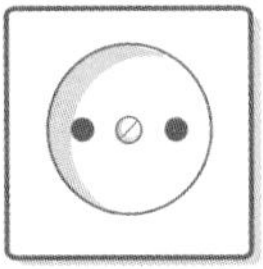

Type C
220-230V/50Hz

Emergencies

Ambulance	061
EU standard emergency number	112
Tourist police	93 256 24 30

Money

The Spanish currency is the euro (€), divided into 100 cents.

ATMs Widely available; there is usually a charge on ATM cash withdrawals abroad.

Cash Banks and building societies offer the best rates; take your passport for ID.

Credit & Debit Cards Accepted in most hotels, restaurants and shops. May need to show passport or an alternative photo ID.

Tipping Catalans typically leave 5% or less at restaurants. Leave more for exceptionally good service. It's rare to leave a tip in bars, though a bit of small change is always appreciated. Tipping taxi drivers is optional, but most locals round up to the nearest euro.

Public Holidays

New Year's Day (Any Nou/Año Nuevo) 1 January

Epiphany/Three Kings' Day (Epifanía or El Dia dels Reis/Día de los Reyes Magos) 6 January

Good Friday (Divendres Sant/Viernes Santo) March/April

Easter Monday (Dilluns de Pasqua Florida) March/April

Labour Day (Dia del Treball/Fiesta del Trabajo) 1 May

Day after Pentecost Sunday (Dilluns de Pasqua Granda) May/June

Dos & Don'ts

Barcelona is fairly relaxed with it comes to etiquette. A few basics to remember:

Greetings Catalans, like other Spaniards, usually greet friends and strangers alike with a kiss on both cheeks, although two males rarely do this. Foreigners may be excused.

Eating and drinking Waiters won't expect you to thank them every time they bring you something, but in more casual restaurants and bars they will expect you to keep your cutlery between courses.

Visiting churches It is considered disrespectful to visit churches as a tourist during Mass and other worship services. Taking photos at such times is a definite no-no.

Escalators Always stand on the right to let people pass, especially when using the metro.

Feast of St John the Baptist (Dia de Sant Joan/Día de San Juan Bautista) 24 June

Feast of the Assumption (L'Assumpció/La Asunción) 15 August

Catalonia's National Day (Diada Nacional de Catalunya) 11 September

Festes de la Mercè 24 September

Spanish National Day (Festa de la Hispanitat/ Día de la Hispanidad) 12 October

All Saints Day (Dia de Tots Sants/Día de Todos los Santos) 1 November

Constitution Day (Día de la Constitución) 6 December

Feast of the Immaculate Conception (La Immaculada Concepció/ La Inmaculada Concepción) 8 December

Christmas (Nadal/ Navidad) 25 December

Boxing Day/St Stephen's Day (El Dia de Sant Esteve) 26 December

Safe Travel

- Violent crime is rare in Barcelona, but petty crime (bag-snatching, pickpocketing) is a major problem.
- You're at your most vulnerable when dragging around luggage to or from your hotel; make sure you know your route before arriving.
- Be mindful of your belongings, particularly in crowded areas.
- Avoid walking around El Raval and the southern end of La Rambla late at night.
- Don't wander down empty city streets at night. When in doubt, take a taxi.
- Take nothing of value to the beach and don't leave anything unattended.

Telephone

Mobile Phones

Local SIM cards are widely available and can be used in European and Australian mobile phones.

US travellers will need to set their phones to roaming, or buy a local mobile and SIM card.

Phone Codes

Country code ☎34

International access code ☎00

Toilets

Public toilets aren't very common in Barcelona. Big shopping centres (or the El Corte Inglés department store) are an option, but ducking into a cafe or bar may be your best bet (it's polite to order something).

Tourist Information

There are several tourist offices around town, including:

Plaça de Catalunya (☎93 285 38 34; www.barcelonaturisme.com; Plaça Catalunya 17; 8.30am-8.30pm; M Catalunya)

Estació Sants (☎93 285 38 34; www.barcelonaturisme.com; Barcelona Sants; 8.30am-8.30pm; Sants Estació)

El Prat Airport (www.barcelonaturisme.com; 8.30am-8.30pm)

Travellers with Disabilities

- Most hotels and public institutions have wheelchair access.
- All buses in Barcelona are wheelchair accessible and a growing number of metro stations are theoretically wheelchair accessible (generally by lift, although there have been complaints that they are only good for people with prams). Of 156 stations, all but 15 are completely adapted (you can check which ones by looking at a network map at: www.tmb.cat/en/transport-accessible).
- Ticket vending machines in metro stations are adapted for disabled travellers, and have Braille options for those a with visual impairment.
- Several taxi companies have adapted vehicles, including **Taxi Amic** (☎93 420 80 88; www.taxi-amic-adaptat.com) and **Green Taxi** (☎900 827900; www.greentaxi.es).
- Most street crossings in central Barcelona are wheelchair-friendly.

Visas

EU & Schengen Countries No visa required.

Australia, Canada, Israel, Japan, New Zealand and the USA No visa required for tourist visits of up to 90 days.

Other Countries Check with a Spanish embassy or consulate.

Language

Both Catalan (*català*) and Spanish (more precisely known as *castellano*, or Castilian) have official language status in Catalonia. In Barcelona you'll hear as much Spanish as Catalan and you'll find that most locals will happily speak Spanish to you, especially once they realise you're a foreigner. In this chapter, we've provided you with some Spanish to get you started, as well as some Catalan basics at the end.

Just read our pronunciation guides as if they were English and you'll be understood. Note that (m/f) indicates masculine and feminine forms.

To enhance your trip with a phrasebook, visit lonelyplanet.com. Lonely Planet iPhone phrasebooks are available through the Apple App store.

Basics

Hello.
Hola. o·la

Goodbye.
Adiós. a·*dyos*

How are you?
¿Qué tal? ke tal

Fine, thanks.
Bien, gracias. byen *gra*·thyas

Please.
Por favor. por fa·*vor*

Thank you.
Gracias. *gra*·thyas

Excuse me.
Perdón. per·*don*

Sorry.
Lo siento. lo *syen*·to

Yes./No.
Sí./No. see/no

Do you speak (English)?
¿Habla (inglés)? a·*bla* (een·*gles*)

I (don't) understand.
Yo (no) entiendo. yo (no) en·*tyen*·do

Eating & Drinking

I'm a vegetarian. (m/f)
Soy vegetariano/a. soy ve·khe·ta·*rya*·no/a

Cheers!
¡Salud! sa·*loo*

That was delicious!
¡Estaba buenísimo! es·*ta*·ba bwe·*nee*·see·mo

Please bring the bill.
Por favor nos trae la cuenta. por fa·*vor* nos *tra*·e la *kwen*·ta

I'd like ...
Quisiera ... kee·*sye*·ra ...

a coffee	*un café*	oon ka·*fe*
a table for two	*una mesa para dos*	*oo*·na *me*·sa *pa*·ra dos
a wine	*un vino*	oon *vee*·no
two beers	*dos cervezas*	dos ther·*ve*·thas

Shopping

I'd like to buy ...
Quisiera comprar ... kee·*sye*·ra kom·*prar* ...

May I look at it?
¿Puedo verlo? *pwe*·do *ver*·lo

How much is it?
¿Cuánto cuesta? *kwan*·to *kwes*·ta

That's too/very expensive.
Es muy caro. es mooy *ka*·ro

Can you lower the price?
¿Podría bajar un poco el precio? po·*dree*·a ba·*khar* oon *po*·ko el *pre*·thyo

Emergencies

Help!
¡Socorro! so·*ko*·ro

Call a doctor!
¡Llame a un médico! *lya*·me a oon *me*·dee·ko

Call the police!
¡Llame a la policía! *lya*·me a la po·lee·*thee*·a

I'm lost. (m/f)
Estoy perdido/a. es·*toy* per·*dee*·do/a

I'm ill. (m/f)
Estoy enfermo/a. es·*toy* en·*fer*·mo/a

Where are the toilets?
¿Dónde están los baños? *don*·de es·*tan* los *ba*·nyos

Time & Numbers

What time is it?
¿Qué hora es? ke *o*·ra es

It's (10) o'clock.
Son (las diez). son (las dyeth)

morning	*mañana*	ma·*nya*·na
afternoon	*tarde*	*tar*·de
evening	*noche*	*no*·che
yesterday	*ayer*	a·*yer*
today	*hoy*	oy
tomorrow	*mañana*	ma·*nya*·na

1	*uno*	*oo*·no
2	*dos*	dos
3	*tres*	tres
4	*cuatro*	*kwa*·tro
5	*cinco*	*theen*·ko
6	*seis*	seys
7	*siete*	*sye*·te
8	*ocho*	*o*·cho
9	*nueve*	*nwe*·ve
10	*diez*	dyeth

Transport & Directions

Where's ...?
¿Dónde está ...? *don*·de es·*ta* ...

What's the address?
¿Cuál es la dirección? kwal es la dee·rek·*thyon*

Can you show me (on the map)?
¿Me lo puede indicar (en el mapa)? me lo *pwe*·de een·dee·*kar* (en el *ma*·pa)

I want to go to ...
Quisiera ir a ... kee·*sye*·ra eer a ...

What time does it arrive/leave?
¿A qué hora llega/sale? a ke *o*·ra *lye*·ga/*sa*·le

I want to get off here.
Quiero bajarme aquí. *kye*·ro ba·*khar*·me a·*kee*

Catalan – Basics

Good morning.
Bon dia. bon *dee*·a

Good afternoon.
Bona tarda. *bo*·na *tar*·da

Good evening.
Bon vespre. bon *bes*·pra

Goodbye.
Adéu. a·*the*·oo

Please.
Sisplau. sees·*pla*·oo

Thank you.
Gràcies. *gra*·see·a

You're welcome.
De res. de res

Excuse me.
Perdoni. par·*tho*·nee

I'm sorry.
Ho sento. oo *sen*·to

How are you?
Com estàs? kom as·*tas*

Very well.
(Molt) Bé. (mol) be

Index

See also separate subindexes for:

Sights 000
Map Pages **000**

Sights 000
Map Pages **000**

Eating

Drinking

Entertainment

Shopping

Sights 000
Map Pages **000**